GLENVIEW PUBLIC LIBRARY

3 1170 00362 6920

D0839242

Walking the Yukon

D

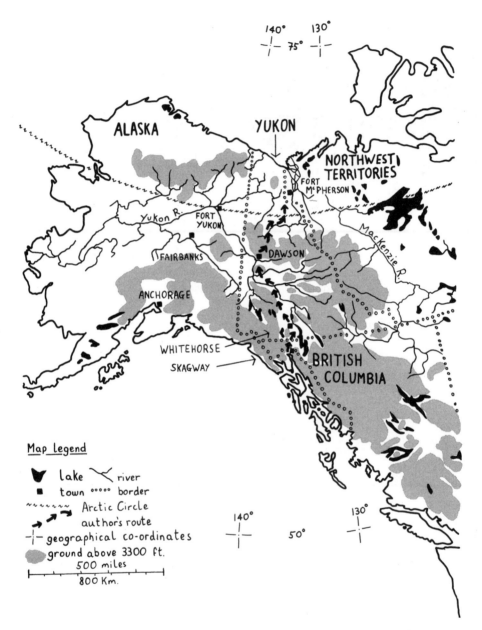

THE YUKON TERRITORY IN RELATION TO NORTHWEST AMERICA

Walking the Yukon

A Solo Trek Through the Land of Beyond

Chris Townsend

Ragged Mountain Press
Camden, Maine

917.191
Tow

Glenview Public Library
1930 Glenview Road
Glenview, Illinois

Published by Ragged Mountain Press

10   9   8   7   6   5   4   3   2

Copyright © 1993 Ragged Mountain Press, an imprint of TAB
Books. TAB Books is a division of McGraw-Hill, Inc.

All rights reserved. The publisher takes no responsibility for the
use of any of the materials or methods described in this book, nor
for the products thereof. The name "Ragged Mountain Press" and
the Ragged Mountain Press logo are trademarks of McGraw-Hill,
Inc. Printed in the United States of America.

Library of Congress Cataloging-in-Publication Data
Townsend, Chris.
Walking the Yukon : a solo trek through the land of beyond /
    Chris Townsend.
p.   cm.
Includes bibliographical references.
ISBN 0-87742-380-6
1. Yukon Territory—Description and travel—1981–2. Townsend,
Chris—Journeys—Yukon Territory. I. Title.
F1091.T68   1994
917.19'1043—dc20   93-9479

Questions regarding the content of this book should be addressed to:
Ragged Mountain Press
P.O. Box 220
Camden, ME 04843

Questions regarding the ordering of this book should be addressed to:
TAB Books/A Division of McGraw-Hill, Inc.
Blue Ridge Summit, PA 17294   1-800-233-1128

A portion of the profits from the sale of each Ragged Mountain
Press book is donated to an environmental cause.

Walking the Yukon is printed on 60-pound Renew Opaque Vellum,
an acid-free paper that contains 50 percent recycled waste paper
(preconsumer) and 10 percent postconsumer waste paper.

Printed by R.R. Donnelley, Harrisonburg, VA.
Design by Joyce C. Weston.
Production and page layout by Molly Mulhern.
Edited by Jonathan Eaton, Dorcas S. Miller, Pamela Benner, and
DeAnna B. Lunden

OCT 13 1994

Contents

Acknowledgments

Many people contributed to my walk in many ways. Without their generous help it would have been much more difficult.

My thanks to:

Denise Thorn, who kept a check on my affairs, answering mail, fielding queries, checking boxes of slides, and more. She also kept the walk going by negotiating a bank overdraft on my behalf and then assuring me I must carry on. Without her it would not have been a success.

Gavin Cullen, manager of the Bank of Scotland in Grantown-on-Spey, who has supported and shown great interest in my rather erratic attempts to make a living out of backpacking.

John Traynor, who made many useful suggestions during the planning of the walk and whose belief in my dreams has always helped me make them come true.

Mike Walsh, for drawing the maps and listening patiently during many late nights to my thoughts and feelings while writing the book.

Ron Billingham and **George Sinfield** of Yukon Tourism, and **Gus Karpes, Lowry Toombs,** and **Red Grossinger** who all gave generously of their time and expertise to help ensure that the walk was a success.

All the people I met along the way, including **Matti Lainema, Erkki Hautaniemi, Alan Sirulnikoff, Danny Roberts, J. Roger Alfred, Dawna Rose, Ian Dowle, Graeme McCahon** and the rest of the Dempster photographers, **Paul Morley,** and **Joe Praner,** for helping make the walk the success it was.

Harald Milz of Akzo and **Gordon Conyers** of Craghoppers for their generous sponsorship. Phoenix Mountaineering, Mountain Equipment, Vasque, Cascade Designs, and RAB Down Equipment for equipment.

The book itself has been a joint production with Ragged Mountain Press, and thanks are due to **Jonathan Eaton, Dorcas Susan Miller, Pamela Benner,** and **DeAnna B. Lunden** for their assistance and useful suggestions.

Thank God! there is always a Land of
Beyond
For us who are true to the trail;
A vision to seek, a beckoning peak,
A fairness that never will fail.
—Robert Service, "The
Land of Beyond"

Introduction

Y ou should try the Yukon next. That's real wilderness." Such
was the response of cargo manager Herb McGilliveray at
Calgary Airport when he heard I was about to spend the summer
walking the length of the Canadian Rockies. At the time I gave his
words no further thought, but more than four months later, as I
approached that journey's end on the Liard River just south of the
Yukon border, the idea of continuing on into the vast romantic
unknown to the north was very appealing. One day, perhaps, I
would return to see if the Yukon lived up to Herb McGilliveray's
praise.

Back home, a couple of months passed before the familiar
urge to start planning a new adventure came on me. The last half of
the Rockies walk had been very tough because of rugged terrain,
lack of trails, and the need to carry more than two weeks' worth of
supplies at a time. Part of me did not want to do another trek like
that. What I thought I wanted was a safe, easy trail walk, not a difficult cross-country wilderness trek, so I toyed with various ideas for

walks in the much more developed mountains of Europe. But none sparked that flash of desire, that surge of excitement that would mean it was what I really wanted to do. At the back of my mind, one name repeated itself insistently: the Yukon, the Yukon, the Yukon. I tried to reject it. "It will mean endless miles of stumbling through tussocky muskeg carrying backbreaking loads," I told myself, but the idea wouldn't go away. It was the only one that stimulated any real interest in me, so almost against my will I found myself studying maps and pondering possible routes. I finally gave in. The Yukon it was to be.

The relief and excitement that accompanied the decision were so great I knew it was the right one. Now I had to organize the walk, no easy task given my minimal knowledge of the Yukon. But it was precisely that sense of the unknown, of a mysterious, little-visited wilderness, that made the project so attractive, however tough it might be. I had for years been entranced by the idea of the Yukon, the myth of the far north. The mere mention of the name conjured images of snowy wastes, vast conifer forests, wolves running silently along frozen rivers, prospectors panning for gold, and trappers hurtling through the wild winter on dogsleds. It was time to go there myself.

1

The Place and the Planning

There's a land where the mountains
are nameless,
And the rivers all run God knows
where

—Robert Service, "The
Spell of the Yukon"

In far northwest Canada lies a great and virtually unknown wilderness: 186,300 square miles of forest, lake, mountain, and tundra split by the great rivers Peel, Porcupine, Pelly, Stewart, and mightiest of all, the Yukon, for which it is named. This is the land of the Klondike gold rush of 1898, the land that inspired Jack London's *Call of the Wild* and the poems of Robert Service—a wild, unspoiled land where grizzly bears and timber wolves still roam free. With a human population of just 29,800, of whom 20,000 live in Whitehorse, the capital city, the Yukon Territory is a land where untouched nature still dominates, a land barely brushed by the twentieth century. There are few such places left.

The Yukon Territory is defined by a mix of natural and political boundaries. On the eastern side the Richardson, Selwyn, and Mackenzie mountain ranges separate the Yukon basin from that of the Mackenzie River in the Northwest Territories; the western boundary is the 141st meridian, dividing Canada from Alaska. Three-quarters of the territory, all but the far north in fact, is drained by the Yukon River.

The southern boundary with British Columbia follows the sixty-degree latitude line, and the northern boundary is the Beaufort Sea, well north of the Arctic Circle at almost seventy degrees. The Yukon is a subarctic land with all the severity of climate that implies. Winters are long and bitter, with temperatures falling tens of degrees below freezing. The lowest temperature ever recorded in Canada was an unbelievably cold minus eighty-one degrees Fahrenheit at Snag, just north of Kluane Lake in the southwest Yukon, in February 1947. In winter there is little daylight for weeks on end, and none at all for a time above the Arctic Circle. The summers, although short, are hot and fairly dry, because the high mountains of the Coast Ranges to the west protect the Yukon from the wet Pacific weather and give it a continental climate. Precipitation during the last ice age was so low that much of the Yukon escaped the glaciation that helped shape the mountains to the south and west. The rounded and smooth appearance of the Yukon's mountains is in part due to this lack of sculpting by ice.

The extreme cold, with annual average temperatures below freezing through much of the region, leads to another distinctive feature: permafrost, or permanently frozen ground. Although not visible, permafrost can be found quickly enough by digging. It is a main cause of the muskeg that covers much of the lower valley and tundra terrain, especially in the northern half of the Yukon. The rock-hard frozen soil is impervious to water, which thus collects on or near the surface despite the scanty precipitation. Permafrost is also one cause of the slow growth of plants in many parts of the Yukon.

The southern Yukon is characterized by its northern coniferous forest with large stands of white and black spruce and smaller ones of lodgepole pine, balsam poplar (cottonwood), aspen, and birch. Timberline is about thirty-five hundred feet. North of Dawson City the forest thins out, giving way to tundra, and muskeg covered with stunted black spruce and tamarack. Larger trees and willow thickets are confined to riverbanks. In the Richardson Mountains, which straddle the Arctic Circle, timberline drops to twenty-five hundred feet; the northern limit of tree growth is just south of the Beaufort Sea. Overall, well over half the Yukon is forested. The animal life of the region includes grizzly and black bears, caribou, moose, wolves, Dall sheep, mountain goats, lynx, wolverine, and beaver. Golden and bald eagles are common.

The Yukon was one of the last places in North America to be explored and settled by Europeans, but one of the first to be inhabited by humans. Perhaps as long as twenty-five thousand years ago, the first Asiatic peoples crossed from Siberia via a land bridge over what is now the Bering Sea to settle in what was to become Alaska and the Yukon. From there they slowly spread south and east to people the continent, until their descendants reached the tip of South America. As successive glacial periods caused sea levels to rise and fall, the land bridge alternately disappeared and reappeared, and there were probably several such migrations, the last being that of the Inuit about ten thousand years ago. Because the central Yukon escaped glaciation, it was habitable at a time when areas farther south were covered by ice.

The memory of the migration from Asia lives on in the legends of the Athapaskan Indians, who make up the bulk of the native peoples of the Yukon. According to their tales, the land bridge was the body of a giant whom one of their ancestors helped to kill. The giant fell into the ocean between Siberia and North America, and Alaska's Aleutian Islands are his last skeletal remains.

The Athapaskans were hunter-gatherers, a migratory people dependent on the seasons and the movement of animals. Of particular importance were the vast herds of caribou, especially the Porcupine herd, which provided skins for clothing and bone for tools as well as meat for food. The natives followed the herds across the Yukon to their winter feeding grounds every autumn and killed them by driving them along lines of sticks into a corral made of branches, where they were easy targets for arrows or spears. A similar system is still used by the Sami of Lapland for trapping the reindeer herds on which they depend, though these herds are now semidomesticated. Reindeer are very closely related to caribou (they look almost the same), so it is rather ironic that the U.S. Congress sent a herd of reindeer with Sami herders to the Yukon in an attempt to relieve food shortages during the gold rush; there were already huge caribou herds in the area.

Fish, especially salmon, were also important to the native people, and one group, the Han, had their main fishing grounds along the Klondike River. Indeed the word *Klondike* derives from the native name Thron-Duick, which means "Hammer Water," as this was the place where stakes were driven into the riverbed to trap migrating salmon. Edible plants, fruits, and berries were gathered, but the natives did not practice agriculture, and being small in number—maybe seven to eight thousand before the first Europeans arrived—they made little impression on the land. The fur traders and trappers also made a minor impact. But the gold rush changed all that, bringing swarms of people and the artifacts of Western industrialism to the Yukon. The native people suffered badly, mostly from epidemic diseases such as smallpox to which they had no resistance, and their numbers fell. The land, though desecrated in places, fared better, as the harshness of the climate and the severity of life in the far north deterred all but the hardiest settlers. This is still one of the greatest wildernesses on earth.

To the experienced hiker the Yukon offers almost endless opportunities for exploration of a type not possible in better-known wilderness regions with their national parks, maintained trails, and backcountry campgrounds. There are no established long routes in the Yukon. Indeed, as far as I could discover, no one had ever set out on a walk such as mine before, a walk done purely for its own sake. Trappers, prospectors, and, in particular, native people have undoubtedly completed longer and tougher treks in the past. One such was that of Scotsman Robert Campbell who, after his Hudson's Bay Company fur trading post at Fort Selkirk, at the confluence of the Yukon and Pelly rivers, was attacked and pillaged by

Chilkat Indians in 1852, walked over three thousand miles on snowshoes through the depths of winter to Lachine, Quebec, to ask permission to rebuild the post. It was an amazing feat of endurance. Unimpressed, the company turned him down.

I would, as always, be going alone. I know well the arguments that solo hiking in a remote wilderness is foolhardy, dangerous, even irresponsible, but I know even more the great rewards that await the lone wanderer, rewards that can hardly be glimpsed by those who walk in groups. Alone I would be able to open myself up to the wilderness, to ready all my senses for what was offered, to learn what the mountains and forests, the rivers and lakes had to teach me. I was not going in order to observe the land from the outside, to view it as a series of picture postcards, but rather to become part of it, to feel that harmony with the natural world that comes only after days alone. This was the real purpose of the walk, and the linking of two points on the map merely an excuse to satisfy the rational part of me and to keep me moving each day. Perhaps one day I'll head out into the wilderness and just sit under a tree for a summer, but for now I need a goal, however distant and hazy.

I feel, anyway, that walking is the best way to gain understanding of a place, to assimilate its rhythms and time scales. All landscapes are dynamic, whether the movement is the infinitesimally slow erosion of a cliff or the swift thunder of an avalanche ripping trees from a hillside. Water and sky move constantly. Life is an essential part of any landscape too—the growth and decay of plants, the flights of birds, migrations of animals. To sit still is to watch the land flow past, to walk is to move with it. Mechanized travel leaves the land behind, disconnecting us from it. One of the problems of modern times is that we are separated from the world that supports us by the speed with which we traverse it. Walking is the best way to know a place, perhaps the only way.

I knew that during the walk I wouldn't often think of finishing. Other long walks had taught me that the night's camp or where to stop for lunch would be the limit of my concerns when I thought ahead at all. The necessity to resupply with food every week or so would break the walk into a series of shorter treks, each valid and unique in its own right.

But why the Yukon, a land so distant? Why not the beautiful Scottish Highlands among which I live, or the Pyrenees, or other easily accessible European mountain ranges? Because of the excitement of not knowing what lies around the next bend, because of a hunger for new vistas and a desire to awake in the wild in a new place each morning. Exploration, discovery, a journey, a pilgrimage—the obsessive wanderer's clichés. That, and a simple pleasure in the physical and mental challenges of journeying in the wild— walking, coping with unknown terrain, camping, evaluating possible routes, choosing river crossings, finding stones to step on and handholds to grasp. Then there are the subtle variations in vegetation, rocks, birds, animals, and, especially, landforms—the infinite number of ways water can move or lie, the infinite forms adopted by mountains, rocks, pebbles at once the same and not the same. All wilderness is one wilderness, yet each is unique. We explore new regions to relearn the old lessons: to have unity there must be diversity, to be connected things must be different.

The possible routes across the Yukon are legion, and the initial problem in planning my walk was one of choice. I knew only that I would walk north, because having the Arctic as my destination would make the walk more fulfilling in an indefinable romantic sense. It just seemed right. I once did a long walk in what felt like the wrong direction. Although I did it for good, sensible reasons, I finished feeling dispirited and with no sense of achievement or pleasure, though most of the walk had been joyous and exciting. Since that anticlimax I have planned walks on aesthetic grounds first, and practicalities second. Luckily, in the Yukon north is the most sensible way to go; it puts the easier walking first and leaves the toughest, remotest country to be tackled when the walker (the term "walk" may sound strange, but to me the trips are long walks rather than hikes, and I am a walker, not a hiker) is better acclimated.

The shape of the Yukon Territory, roughly a tall right triangle, made a south-north route seem the most obvious. A closer look at the map, however, showed that the mountain ranges trend mostly from southeast to northwest, as the Yukon is situated where the south-north ranges of the Lower Forty-eight and British Columbia are deflected westward into Alaska.

The most obvious pure mountain route would start in the southeast, run northwestward through the Mackenzie and Selwyn mountains along the border with the Northwest Territories, then curve west through the Wernecke and Ogilvie ranges. This route was attempted on skis by a party led by British army officer Guy Sheridan in 1986 and described in his book *Tales of a Cross Country Skier.* On that trip supplies were cached every 125 to 175 miles by helicopter and by trappers heading into the mountains for the winter. The team planned on doing fifteen to twenty miles a day, but on foot in summer and without being able to share the weight of my camping gear, I knew I would be lucky to average anything near that mileage. Ten to twelve miles a day seemed more feasible. (In fact, Sheridan's party was hampered by equipment failure and difficult snow conditions. They ended up making three separate trips and barely covering half their intended route.)

I studied this eastern Yukon route longingly. The idea of spending weeks alone in pristine wilderness was very appealing, but I had to concede that I lacked the resources to attempt such a remote trek requiring frequent and expensive resupply by air. Then too, such a journey would pass by all the areas of historical interest in the Yukon. As I read the leaflets and brochures that trickled back from my inquiries to governmental departments and tourist bureaus, I realized that the history of the gold rush and other recent events important to the identity of the Yukon—such as the stories of the Mad Trapper of Rat River and the Lost Patrol—are still traceable on the ground. I began to list the places I wanted to visit for their historical importance as well as their scenic or wilderness qualities.

In Kluane National Park, in the southwest Yukon adjacent to

Alaska's Wrangell–Saint Elias National Park, is 19,845-foot Mount Logan, Canada's highest peak, along with the world's largest non-polar ice fields. The softer, unglaciated eastern edges of the park contain many trails and are the most popular hiking area in the Yukon. Starting there would give me easy walking for the first few weeks—always a good way to begin a long trek—and magnificent alpine scenery. Having abandoned the mountain route to the east, I worked out a more complex route crossing the grain of the land from Kluane northward to finish in the Richardson Mountains, well north of the Arctic Circle. This route would enable me to cross and recross the Yukon's sparse road network, making resupply easier and cheaper, and it would take me through the Klondike goldfields and Dawson City, places I wanted to visit. Finally, it would allow me to walk for several days along the banks of the Yukon River.

Long hours of poring intently over the three 1:1,000,000 topographic maps that cover the Yukon produced a basic outline of a route, which I then traced in more detail onto larger-scale 1:250,000 maps. The dozens of 1:50,000 maps needed for the actual walking would have to be picked up in Whitehorse. There was a limit to how much material it was practical to transport across the Atlantic! I knew anyway that the bold yellow lines I was happily scoring across the maps would only slightly resemble my eventual route, for the maps couldn't tell me what the ground underfoot would be like. Because hiking in the Yukon outside of Kluane is virtually nonexistent, I was unable to find out much about the terrain outside the park, though what little information I did glean was not encouraging. Much of the walk, as I had originally suspected, was likely to consist of bushwhacking through dense forest and slogging through the tussocks and water-filled holes of muskeg. It did appear, however, that there were many long-abandoned trappers' and prospectors' trails, and these, if I could locate them, might in places mitigate the severity of the terrain. Even so, I planned on averaging only twelve miles a day. Of course, part of the excitement of planning and undertaking this walk was not knowing what the country was like or what would lie over the next hill or around the next river bend.

I based my planning in the winter of 1989–1990 on the route north from Kluane, only to change it a few weeks before my departure when I discovered the Chilkoot Trail. This trail runs north from the Pacific Ocean through the Coast Ranges of southeast Alaska and British Columbia, and was the route into the Yukon used by most of the 1898 Klondike gold rush stampeders. It seemed appropriate to begin a walk through the Yukon through this historic gateway, even though it meant starting not only outside the Yukon but even outside Canada. I wrestled hard with the decision. Kluane looked attractive, but because it lies well to the west of the Chilkoot Trail, linking them on a south-north walk wasn't feasible. I had to choose between the two. When I worked out that the beginning on the Chilkoot would allow me to follow roughly the route of the Klondikers all the way to the goldfields, the issue was decided. The first third of my route shifted eastward, though the rest stayed the same.

I planned my route around the logistics of resupply, always the most difficult part of any wilderness trek. From previous experience I knew I would need around two pounds dry weight of food per day. My basic pack weight would be around forty pounds, and I would be carrying ten pounds of camera gear, so I would need to resupply frequently to keep the total load as low as possible. But I also wanted to venture as far from roads and settlements as I could. Two weeks' food was the maximum I could consider carrying, and that was really too much for enjoyable walking. My plan—the one I left home with but expected to alter once I had talked to people in Whitehorse and also during the walk itself—involved eight food drops at post offices, highway maintenance camps, and hotels. The most food I would have to carry would be fifteen days' worth, a horrific thirty pounds, while twice I would set off with thirteen-day supplies. On the other hand, I would start the trek with just five days' food and enjoy the same light load on three other sections.

My planning also had to take into account the short northern summer. The deep snow that lies high in the Coast Ranges along the Alaska-Canada border well into summer would prevent my starting before mid-June, and I needed to finish by mid-September, when the first snows start falling in the Richardson Mountains. My chosen route was roughly a thousand miles long, which I estimated would take about three months when rest days, essential on a long trek, were taken into account. There was just enough time, if no major problems arose.

Most of my information on the Yukon was provided by Yukon Tourism via the Canadian High Commission Tourism Section in London. Ron Billingham, then Yukon Tourism's publicity officer, was clearly concerned about my plans. In one letter to the High Commission he wrote: "The northern Yukon is very sparsely populated, and many areas are accessible only in the winter. . . . I strongly urge Mr. Townsend to obtain firsthand information on the conditions from one of our experienced bush guides." This seemed sensible advice, so I sent copies of my route to three wilderness tour companies. I received only one reply, but it was enough. "Your route," wrote David Howe of Rainbow Tours, "looks feasible." That was what I wanted to hear. He also suggested I seek up-to-date information on river levels and ground conditions when I arrived in the Yukon. This also seemed a good idea. I had given no consideration to either of these important factors in my planning, for the simple reason that I had no information on them at all.

Thus it was with only a sketchy idea of the route I would take and what the walk would entail that I left home on June 11 for a forty-two-hour journey via Glasgow, Chicago, Seattle, and Vancouver to Whitehorse. The endless round of airports and airplanes left me numbed and exhausted, though I rallied a little when the snow-covered mountains of northern British Columbia came into view during the final few hours of the last flight. I was glad to set foot in Whitehorse and the Yukon and know that soon the real traveling would begin.

First, though, there were final arrangements and the inevitable last-minute hitches to be dealt with. I didn't know yet what the hitches were, but I knew there would be some. There always are. I planned on spending three or four days in Whitehorse before starting the walk. I just hoped whatever problems emerged wouldn't be too serious.

Ron Billingham met me at the airport and whisked me off to a bar for a first taste of Canadian beer and a blurred, confused meeting with several people who, when I was introduced as an Englishman intent on walking the length of the Yukon, made clear what they thought of my sanity. Weary from travel, I was relieved, later in the evening, to sink onto the bed in my room in the Regina Hotel, provided courtesy of Yukon Tourism. But the hassles had already started. The best specialty backpacking food I know of is made by the California company AlpineAire, so I had ordered my supplies from them and asked that they be sent straight to Whitehorse. Two large boxes had arrived, which was good news—except that there should have been three.

I was too tired to stay awake worrying that night, but early the next morning I phoned AlpineAire. A bright, cheerful California voice answered the phone, though the news it gave was more in keeping with my usual early-morning state of mind. The missing box had just been returned to AlpineAire, sent back by Canada Post as "too large," though it was no bigger than one of those that had reached me, I was assured. "I need the food now," I spluttered. "I want to start walking in a few days." "We'll find the quickest way to get it to you and call you back," she said. A few hours later the phone rang. At least nine days, they said. I was speechless. Nine days! Val of the Regina Hotel suggested I advise AlpineAire to try Canadian Airlines, which had daily flights to Whitehorse, but when I rang California again, AlpineAire had worked out a complex scheme involving the United Parcel Service that would get the box to me in five days. I could just about live with this, not that it seemed I had any choice. Unfortunately, the missing box contained all my main meals; the ones that had arrived held breakfast cereal, lunch bars, and packet soups.

In the meantime I had people to meet and a town to explore. Before making the round of the tourist attractions, I trekked out to the Northern Affairs Program map office where the manager, Beth Philips, had my 1:50,000 maps waiting. But the list I'd sent had been for the Kluane route, so I needed to change some of them. Beth was very patient as I spread maps all over the counter, trying to work out which I needed and which I didn't. Eventually I left, clutching what I hoped were the right ones.

Whitehorse is brash and modern, though with many traces of its pioneer origins, such as the SS *Klondike,* a beached, renovated sternwheeler from the days when river travel was the Yukon's main transportation. Those days only ended in the 1950s, when the highway system was built. Much of my time in town I spent in the two bookshops, Macs Fireweed and Books on Main, browsing for books about the Yukon and the North. I also visited the Macbride Museum, housed in a rustic log cabin, but I wasn't enthusiastic. It wasn't the town's fault, but a reflection of my mood. I was just passing time, waiting impatiently for the walk to begin. The weather didn't help. It rained, heavily and constantly.

I did seize the opportunity during a brief break in the downpour to take a short eight-mile round trip on the wide, placid but powerful, forest-fringed Yukon River aboard Red Grossinger's *Youcon Kat,* a commercial flat-bottomed riverboat that, though I didn't know it at the time, was to play an important part in the walk at a later date. The main interest of the tour was bird life. "Raven, sandpiper, gulls, ducks, sand swallows, and a belted kingfisher," I wrote in my journal. But the highlights of the trip were the eagles. At one point Red swung the boat into the bank. High above, an untidy mass of sticks in a dead tree marked a bald eagle's nest. Two magnificent eagles, their distinctive white heads making identification easy, were perched nearby, completely uninterested in the excited group of people watching them through binoculars from below. Farther downstream a golden eagle sat motionless on a snag jutting out of the water, surveying the river as it rushed by, and another did the same from atop a tree on the bank. Four eagles within the confines of Whitehorse; the birdwatching possibilities looked exciting. I was glad I had brought a pair of 8 x 21 mini-binoculars, despite their five ounces of additional weight.

On my second evening in Whitehorse, I was invited to dinner by George Sinfield, whose upright bearing betrayed the fact that he was a retired British army officer (though a Canadian by birth and nationality), even if his luxuriant bushy mustache rather implied the Royal Air Force. George worked for Yukon Tourism as a policy analyst. Several other people were there, including experienced river guide Gus Karpes, the author of several books on the Yukon's rivers. He advised me to change the middle section of my route, as it involved crossing two large and unfordable rivers, the Pelly and the Stewart. His suggestion was that I stick to the west bank of the Yukon, where there were some trails, a few remote habitations, and only one big river to cross—the White, which might be passable on foot. If not, the Yukon carried enough boat traffic that I should be able to find a lift quite easily.

It seemed unwise to ignore the advice of a local expert, especially one whose quiet but firm tones, wiry muscled body, and worn, wilderness-hewn face spoke of authority and knowledge. I decided to follow Gus's suggestion despite the fact that it would leave me a 260-mile section with no opportunity to resupply. At twelve miles a day that would mean an impossibly heavy twenty-one days' worth of food, and to bring that down to a merely back-breaking two weeks' worth, I would have to average eighteen miles a day—an impossibility in really rugged trackless terrain. As I wrote in my journal later that evening, "If trails are good I could do it. I think I'll try." The next day I bought a copy of Gus's *Upper Yukon River,* Volume Two, *Carmacks to Dawson River,* which, though intended for canoe travelers, contained useful information on campsites as well as interesting snippets of history. I'd been uncomfortably aware of Gus's piercing gaze at George's get-together. I felt that he was assessing me, trying to work out whether this British newcomer, who had never been to the Yukon before, was really capable of walking the length of the land. His look alone gave me a great deal to live up to.

Five days after my arrival in Whitehorse, the missing food box had progressed northward a second time, but only as far as Vancouver. AlpineAire rang to say it would take several days more; apparently UPS planes went no farther north, so the package was to be transshipped by truck. My journal expresses my reaction succinctly: "Damn!" Ron Billingham came to the rescue and spent an afternoon ringing UPS to try to get them to transfer the box to a plane. In the meantime I decided I would leave the next day anyway, and with that in mind I prowled the aisles of a Whitehorse supermarket for extra food, emerging with several packets of macaroni and cheese, ramen noodles, and Minute Rice, plus cheese and margarine, enough, I hoped, to keep me fed each evening of the ten-day return walk to Whitehorse.

I wasn't starting out with ten days' food, however, as halfway back to Whitehorse I would pass through the little settlement of Carcross. There was no store in Carcross, but Lowry Toombs, Parks Canada's manager of the SS *Klondike*—another person I'd met at George Sinfield's very useful dinner party—had offered to take supplies to Carcross for me, as he lived nearby. On the morning of June 19 I dropped off a stuff sack of food at the SS *Klondike* before departing for Skagway, Dyea, and the Chilkoot Trail in a Yukon government car courtesy of Yukon Tourism and George Sinfield, who was driving. The rest of my food resided in George's house, packed into boxes and bags and just awaiting the addition of the missing meals before being sealed and dispatched.

As we headed south into Alaska on the South Klondike Highway I felt my first doubts about the trip. The wilderness outside looked so vast and so alien. Am I overreaching myself? I wondered. I was a little scared, and it barely registered that I was finally in Alaska, an almost mythical place I had been longing to visit for years.

Dropping rapidly down from the border posts on White Pass among the imposing snow-streaked peaks of the Coast Range, we reached Skagway. Although an American town, Skagway is essentially the Yukon's port, and the road to Whitehorse is the only one out of the narrow, mountain-rimmed valley in which it lies. It was the Klondike gold rush that brought people here in enough numbers for a town to develop.

Originally called Mooresville by Captain William Moore, who staked out a town site here in 1888, Skagway was renamed by the first stampeders when they invaded the shores of Skagway Bay in 1897. The name comes from the Tlingit Indian word *skagus,* which means "home of the north wind." Moore's claims to the land were ignored by the stampeders, though he did eventually win his case through the courts and in the meantime made a fortune from the wharf he'd built on the tidal mud flats.

With no police or legal authority, Skagway was a frontier town of the most lawless, violent sort. Gunplay was common, and many reports of the time characterized the place as a hellhole. Remote and difficult to reach, Skagway attracted criminals and outlaws who had worn out their welcome in more civilized places. Chief among these was Jefferson Randolph Smith, otherwise known as Soapy and probably the single most famous character of the gold rush. His gang pretty much ruled the town between the summers of 1897 and 1898, fleecing newcomers of their money and supplies in rigged card games and sometimes using murder and robbery to achieve their ends. Yet Soapy Smith cultivated the persona of a polite man who contributed to churches and established a pound to care for stray dogs, among other charitable works.

Eventually Soapy's gang robbed a prospector who wasn't too scared to speak out, and the tide turned. A vigilante group called the Committee of 100 was formed to protect the town from the gang, and the result was a gunfight between one of the vigilantes, Frank

Reid, and Soapy Smith himself. Smith was killed outright, and Reid died of his wounds two weeks later. Today Smith's grave is a popular tourist spot.

Nowadays it is the romance of the Klondike that keeps Skagway in existence, as tourists pour in to savor the restored 1898 atmosphere. Most come by cruise ship, for the town lies at the end of a long, deep fjord called the Lynn Canal and is the terminus of the world-famous Inside Passage journey from Seattle. It is startling to see the huge oceangoing ships docked in the narrow channel with glacier-clad mountains towering on either side. With its wooden boardwalks, frame-fronted stores, and dirt roads, Skagway is an interesting place, but I found it rather overcrowded and noisy. After visiting the National Historical Park Visitor Center to learn details of current conditions on the Chilkoot Trail, George and I left town for the eight-mile drive to the trailhead. En route we passed two groups of heavily laden walkers, the second being a pair whose green cotton clothing and knee-high rubber boots proclaimed Scandinavian origins. One of them had a small ax strapped to his pack, indicating they were going farther than the Chilkoot Trail, on which fires aren't allowed.

Early that afternoon George dropped me off beside the Taiya River and started back to Whitehorse. I was alone, and the walk was finally about to begin.

2

In the Footsteps of the Gold Rush: The Chilkoot Trail

DYEA TO CARCROSS

JUNE 19–24, 58 MILES

It was a hard day's run, up the canon, through Sheep Camp, past the Scales and the timber line, across glaciers and snowdrifts hundreds of feet deep, and over the great Chilkoot Divide, which stands between the salt water and the fresh and guards forbiddingly the sad and lonely North.

—Jack London, *The Call of the Wild*

Standing on the windswept banks of the Taiya River, I found it hard to imagine that Dyea was once home to four thousand people and host to thousands of gold seekers en route to the Klondike. The bedlam, the crowds, the constant stream of people and animals laden with all manner of goods trudging up to the pass are gone now. The town itself, apparently a far pleasanter place than Skagway, is gone as well, and all is quiet; the forests, mountains, and mud flats are as they were before three men struck gold on a remote creek far to the north. It is reassuring to see how quickly nature can reclaim a ravaged area, how soon the signs of man can be obliterated. No longer is the Chilkoot trailhead a "nest of ants taken into a strange country and stirred up by a stick," as John Muir put it. Muir had visited southeast Alaska three times before the gold rush and wrote of the Lynn Canal in his book *Travels in Alaska:* "The mountains on either hand and at the head of the canal are strikingly beautiful at any time of year." It is good that they still are.

"GOLD! GOLD! GOLD! GOLD!" ran the *Seattle-Post Intelligencer*'s headline for July 17, 1897, the day the first gold

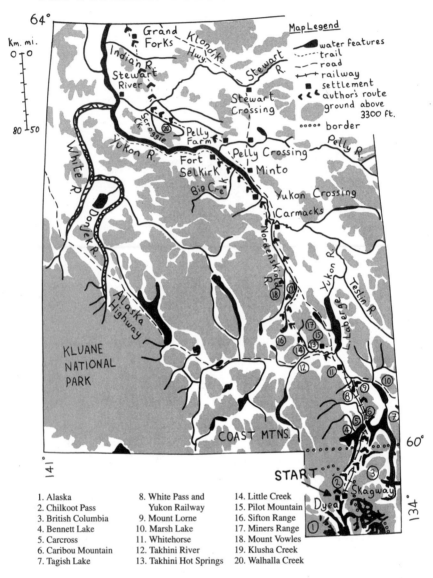

1. Alaska
2. Chilkoot Pass
3. British Columbia
4. Bennett Lake
5. Carcross
6. Caribou Mountain
7. Tagish Lake
8. White Pass and Yukon Railway
9. Mount Lorne
10. Marsh Lake
11. Whitehorse
12. Takhini River
13. Takhini Hot Springs
14. Little Creek
15. Pilot Mountain
16. Sifton Range
17. Miners Range
18. Mount Vowles
19. Klusha Creek
20. Walhalla Creek

from the Klondike arrived in Seattle aboard the steamer *Portland*. A day earlier another vessel laden with gold, the *Excelsior*, had docked in San Francisco. The last great gold rush was on. The actual discovery was on August 17, 1896, but so remote was the Klondike that the gold took nearly a year to reach the outside world, though rumors of the strike had by then caused many would-be miners to hurry north. Their numbers were nothing compared with those that set off in the summer and autumn of 1897, spurred on by massive press coverage, dreams of riches, and the excitement of participation in a great adventure.

Although many routes were promoted as the best way to reach the Klondike, a place no one had heard of before, only three were really feasible. The most comfortable but expensive way, known as the rich man's route, was by coastal steamer to St. Michael, Alaska, and then up the Yukon to the Klondike by riverboat, the route by which, in reverse, the first successful miners had brought out their gold. The majority, however, had to make their own way to the goldfields, and the routes most of them chose were via the Chilkoot and White passes in southeast Alaska, because these involved the least overland travel, with just thirty or so miles of mountains to be crossed before reaching the headwaters of the Yukon River, down which they could float to the goldfields.

Those who could afford to hire pack animals went by White Pass; those who couldn't, by far the greater number, went via the Chilkoot Pass, an old Indian trading route that had already been in use by prospectors for more than a decade. Both routes led to Lake Bennett, where the stampeders spent the winter of 1898 building crude boats to take them down the Yukon to the Klondike as soon as the spring breakup occurred.

The Chilkoot Pass route was used heavily for only one winter, as by February 1899 the opening of the White Pass and Yukon railroad made travel from Skagway into the Yukon interior easy. As quickly as it had become a major thoroughfare, the Chilkoot route faded into oblivion. The trees grew back, the shanty towns slowly rotted, the cable systems collapsed onto the rocks, the wilderness reclaimed its own. But during the stampede the trail was in constant use, tramped by heavily loaded people and pack animals, for every gold seeker was required to bring a year's worth of supplies into Canada, an amount known as the "ton of goods." Few supplies were available in the interior of the Yukon, and the authorities had a genuine fear that the sudden inrush of "miners," many of them totally inexperienced in wilderness travel and survival, would lead to deaths from cold and starvation.

The "ton of goods" requirement was enforced by a detachment of North West Mounted Police—the original Mounties, later to become the Royal Canadian Mounted Police—who camped atop the pass during the bitter winter of 1898 checking loads and charging duty. Stampeders moved supplies in relays from one cache point to the next; it is estimated they walked the thirty miles from Dyea to Bennett up to sixty times before they had transported all their goods. Only those who could afford to pay packers—often local natives who carried phenomenal weights (one took a 350-pound barrel over the pass)—hire horses or mules, or pay for goods to be taken up by the aerial tramways that were soon built could shorten this eighteen-hundred-mile trek through the extreme winter cold and deep snows of the Coast Mountains.

The primary purpose of the police post on the Chilkoot Pass was to establish once and for all the border between the United States and Canada. Until the gold rush it had never been clearly delineated and was still in dispute. The United States said the border lay east of the mountains at the headwaters of the Yukon River, while Canada claimed all the land right down to the sea at Skagway and Dyea. Eventually conceding the coastline to the Americans, the Canadian government opted for the watershed of the Coast Range as the border and hence decided to man the mountain passes, of which the Chilkoot was by far the most important. Another police detachment was established at White Pass. By charging customs duty, the police were firmly establishing the international boundary. Just in case anybody objected, they also set up a Maxim machine gun to guard their new frontier.

The Mounties atop the Chilkoot Pass also marked the boundary between the lawless pioneer towns of southeast Alaska, and Canada, where the law was strictly enforced. Once over the pass the stampeders were under the paternalistic eye of the incorruptible and legendary Superintendent Sam Steele of the NWMP, a stickler for discipline and order. No longer need they fear the predations of the Soapy Smith gang or any other criminals. "They would not show their faces in the Yukon," said Steele.

As interest in the gold-rush days grew and tourism became important for both Skagway and the Yukon in the 1960s, the overgrown stampeder's trail was cleared and reopened as a hiking route that became part of the Klondike Gold Rush National Historical Park in the 1970s, run jointly by the park services of the United States and Canada. Now the route is popular once more, with hundreds of hikers making the trek every year. To ensure that today's modern adventurers don't wreak the destruction of those of yesteryear, the trail is maintained and patrolled by park service rangers. Designated campgrounds with outhouses and shelter cabins have been established to minimize impact.

As well as being a beautiful wilderness in its own right, the Chilkoot Trail is also "the longest museum in the world," with relics of the gold rush evident on every side and interpretative signboards showing how it would have been when it was the "Trail of '98." The mix of industrial archaeology and mountain grandeur makes it a unique walk, fascinating in its contradictions, and I was looking forward to following in the wake of the Klondikers as I began my journey north.

Staring out across the still estuary at Dyea, I wondered what it must have been like during the gold rush when the boats and bustle disturbed the quiet waters. Then, like the Klondikers before me, I turned my back on the misty tidal flats and took my first steps toward the Yukon. I felt a strange mixture of serenity and exhilaration. The problems of planning, the anticipation and worry were suddenly gone, to be replaced by immediacy of purpose, a realization that now only the next few hours mattered and the world consisted solely of the forest, the river, and the mountains. I breathed out deeply and smiled, confidence restored.

The trail undulated upward through the lush coastal forest, a dark brown line threading through the greenery. Bright flowers lined the way, along with huge head-high, poison-spined devil's club. Grouse exploded noisily from the undergrowth, while from high in the trees the pure, single note of the varied thrush rang out. Fresh bear dung showed I was back in real wilderness and had me calling out my presence just in case the animal itself was over the next rise. The clouds hung low and thick over the mountaintops, but occasionally they parted to show massive gray-white glaciers tumbling down above steep forested slopes. The weather in these mountains is usually wet and cloudy, raked as they are by a constant stream of storms coming off the Pacific.

Three hours and eight miles later I reached Canyon City. Here at the mouth of the Taiya River canyon is a natural campsite, a stopover point for Indian traders and early prospectors long before the gold rush caused a log-cabin village to spring up, a transient settlement that had vanished by the end of 1898. Now there is just one shelter cabin for hikers, inside which I cooked my first meal before pitching my tent beside the rushing waters of the Taiya. I could have slept in the cabin, but on this, the first night of the trek, I wanted to sleep in the tent. The notes I wrote in my journal that evening show the doubt and worry that always disturb me during the first few days of a long walk, only to disappear once a daily routine is established: "Pack felt heavy but not too much, . . . soles of feet very sore and hot, . . . still it is the first day. . . . I'm working out what I can drop off at Whitehorse . . . tarp? . . . half of paracord?"

The cabin contained a woodstove, which I didn't light. It was dry and not at all cold—sixty degrees Fahrenheit, according to the small maximum-minimum thermometer I carried. I found in the cabin interesting personal accounts of traveling the trail during the gold rush, and information on the wildlife of the area. I was reading these when the first of the evening's visitors called in, an olive-green-clad ranger heading down to Dyea. "The weather looks good the other side of the pass," were his encouraging parting words. Then three more figures trooped in and announced that they were archaeologists who had just been flown in by helicopter to the historic Canyon City town site, across the river, where they would be spending the summer working.

Once they had gone I pondered the ranger's words and considered my plans for the morrow. The Chilkoot Pass itself is at the top of a very steep rocky slope known to the stampeders as the Golden Stairs. At 3,739 feet it's well above timberline and notorious for bad weather. "Wet foggy weather conditions are present in the area of the pass 60 to 80 percent of the time," said the notes in the Canadian Parks Service 1990 Chilkoot Trail Information Package I'd picked up in Whitehorse. Beyond the pass the trail stayed above timberline for eight miles and was still mostly snowbound, according to the latest reports. The weather and the snow didn't concern me overmuch. If I couldn't cope with such conditions on a well-marked trail, the chances of my completing the whole walk were slight. But I did want to see the pass itself and the country beyond. I decided I would cross the pass the next day if the weather was clear; otherwise, I'd spend a second night in Alaska.

I woke frequently during the night—whenever there was the slightest noise, in fact. It would take me a few nights to grow used to sleeping in bear country again and learn to distinguish between rain splattering on the fly sheet, the wind in the trees, the scurryings of small animals, fish jumping in the river, and the solid, heavier sounds of large mammals. The rain I heard each time I woke had stopped by morning, and through the tall trees that enclosed the site I could see a few small patches of blue.

A few showers accompanied me as I plodded up through the forest, accompanied by birdsong and delighting in the magnificent trees, especially the huge balsam poplars, and the luxuriant and bright, well-watered vegetation. A flash of moving color caught my eye, and I turned to watch a beautiful red-headed woodpecker watching me. I saw more bear sign, including boulders with the moss raked off, so I again made sure any bears that might be ahead could hear me coming.

After two and a half hours I reached Sheep Camp, so named by mountain-sheep hunters who had used it as a base. As the last sheltered flat spot before the final push to the pass, it became an important stopping point during the gold rush. At one point it had a population of six to eight thousand. Accommodation, food, and entertainment were provided in tents and log shelters by those Klondikers intending to set up businesses rather than search for gold.

Sheep Camp serves the same purpose for hikers as it once did for the stampeders, the next campsite being the small and unprotected—and ill-named—Happy Camp four miles beyond the top of the pass. I had lunch inside the shelter cabin, still intending to cross the pass that day. But by 1:00 P.M. the clouds had darkened and dropped down the mountainside, and it was pouring rain. The five-day-old trail report pinned up in the shelter read: "Extensive snow-fields ½ mile south of the Scales. . . . Thinning snow can be hazardous. . . . Trail covered with snow almost completely from the Chilkoot Summit to Happy Camp. . . . An early start (by 8–10 A.M.) advised." I decided that perhaps I would stay. The cabin, much lighter inside than the rather somber one at Canyon City, was warm and cozy. Why go outside, get soaked, and see nothing? I thought. A hummingbird hovered outside a window, its blurred wings matching the steadily falling rain.

Later in the afternoon two other walkers arrived, the pair in faded green cotton clothing and rubber boots I had passed on the road from Skagway to Dyea. They were, as I had surmised, from Scandinavia—Finland, in fact. Even so, Matti Lainema and Erkki Hautaniemi were veterans of many Alaskan adventures, both on foot and by canoe, their original inspiration being the stories of Jack

London. Like me, they intended to continue their walk all the way to Whitehorse, but from there they planned to canoe the rest of the way to Dawson City.

Their gear was wet with rain, so the Finns set about to light the woodstove. After splitting ready-cut pine logs with their hand ax, they quickly sliced "feather-sticks" for tinder with the long sharp Lapp knives both wore on their belts. The speed of the operation showed they were adept at this.

Since wood fires aren't allowed on the Chilkoot Trail, Matti and Erkki carried a Trangia alcohol stove, the standard backpacking stove in Scandinavia, plus a very small amount of marine stove fuel they had bought in Skagway. In order to keep the weight of their packs down, they carried a daily ration of only twelve hundred calories' worth of food. They planned on catching fish once down from the mountains. "Erkki will feel the lack of food before me," said Matti, laughing, "I've got plenty of fat to burn off." Neither of them looked unfit to me. Matti was the taller, but both were muscular and strong, with lined, weather-beaten faces that spoke of years of wilderness wandering.

The stove in the cabin was made from a round drum on which balancing a pan was impossible, so Matti and Erkki had to use their camp stove and precious fuel to produce their meal. Soon steam was rising both from their pan and from the wet clothing hanging around the cabin, creating a humid but warm and homey atmosphere.

"The Chilkoot is not a wilderness hike. You will share the trail with many other hikers," said the notes on the back of the Parks Service trail map, though they did go on to say that mid-July to mid-August was the busiest time. There were plenty of folk trying to beat the rush, two more of whom arrived late in the afternoon, one of them a ranger from Glacier Bay National Park taking a busman's holiday. They had come over the pass from the north and reported that on top it was wet and very windy, with thick mist eliminating visibility. After a quick brew-up and a partial drying out of their clothes, they went on down, intending to spend the night at

Canyon City. Outside, the downpour continued, though the clouds did lift briefly to reveal the edge of a glacier high on the mountainside above the cabin.

The next visitor was Scott, the resident summer ranger, who had a cabin nearby. He warned us about the danger of collapsing snow bridges beyond the summit and brought the unwelcome news that the rain was meant to worsen the next day. Looking outside, I found it hard to believe this could be possible. As I intended to move on regardless of the weather, it being far too early in the walk for a day off, especially after two half days, I made my preparations for the next day, writing in my journal: "Tomorrow will wear long johns + rain pants + thick thermal sweater + rain jacket if still wet." I was clearly not yet feeling confident about being a full-time backpacker, as I also wrote: "My new bright-red, green, and blue Cloudbreaker jacket looks very 'unserious' compared with the Finns' battered green cotton jackets." Virtually all my gear was brand new, making me feel like a novice. It would take a couple of weeks before it began to feel worn in and "right" and developed a trail patina. By then, I hoped, *I* would feel trail hardened as well.

Before retreating to their tent for the night, the Finns offered me a cup of coffee. I took a mouthful and gasped, shocked by the powerful bitter taste as the wave of caffeine hit me. I'd been warned by their comments about all coffee in the United States being "dishwater" to expect something strong, but nothing had prepared me for the effects of two large dessert spoonfuls of freeze-dried coffee dissolved in about half an inch of boiling water in the bottom of a cup. I decided I much preferred to drink dishwater!

Kept awake by the coffee, I sat by myself in the cabin reading more stories from the gold-rush days and watching a couple of very bold mice scuttling about on the floor. With the fire lit, the temperature was seventy degrees Fahrenheit. Outside it was cold, wet, and windy, and I had no desire to make even the short trek to my tent. At 11:00 P.M. I was just making the effort to move, the fire having died down and the temperature dropping, when two sodden hikers burst through the door, their denim shorts, thin "waterproof" tops, and lightweight footwear very inappropriate for the conditions. As I was rebuilding the fire, they told me they were on an Inside Passage cruise and were not really walkers at all. They had set off on the hike on the misunderstanding, apparently gained from the ranger in Dyea, that there was a highway at the top of the pass from which they could hitchhike a return. Scott, whom they had just been talking to, had disabused them of this notion. Now they knew what was really involved, they had sensibly decided to go back down the next day. Although wet and tired, they were, they said, enjoying this brief wilderness trek.

The two late arrivals still slept in their tent when I set off the next morning about half an hour behind the Finns. The sky was overcast, but the rain had stopped and the clouds were lifting. As the trail climbed out of the forest the high rocky peaks and tumbling white glaciers that walled in the narrow valley came into view, a grand, wild sight. Eventually, after much meandering through boulder and talus fields, the trail arrived at the flat area known as the Scales, so called for the weighing of gold-rush goods in order to set a rate for packing or hoisting them over the pass. It was also the final cache for goods before the steep climb to the pass, a climb that caused many people to abandon anything they could do without. As at other stopping points, makeshift saloons, bunkhouses, and restaurants sprang up to serve the migrant community. And, as elsewhere on the trail, artifacts from the time—everything from decaying leather shoes to large rusting boilers—litter the ground. These are now protected, and it is illegal to disturb them or take them away, a peculiar fate for the garbage of a previous age.

From the Scales the final eight-hundred-foot climb leads up steep boulder slopes to a narrow notch in the mountain wall. Beyond it lies Petterson Pass, down which swept a high avalanche on Palm Sunday, 1898, killing more than sixty people. This is a famous view, immortalized in the photographs of Eric Hegg and others that show an unbroken black line of heavily laden men angling up the white snowfields into the sky, pictures that symbol-ize the gold rush and all the hardship it entailed. Throughout the Yukon this image is to be found, and it always means one thing, the Klondike, even though it was taken far away and in another coun-try. Staring up at the steep slopes, I found it hard to imagine what it must have been like in 1898 in the savage cold of an Alaskan win-ter to look up at that climb and know you would have to undertake it as many as thirty times in order to get all your goods to the top.

For me, who had to do it only once and with a relatively light load, the climb, mostly on snow, was strenuous but not difficult. The steepest angle is about forty-five degrees. It is probably much harder later in the season, when the snow is gone. Beside the route, marked by orange poles, lie remnants of aerial tramways and pul-leys. Looking back as I paused near the top of the climb, I could see Matti and Erkki, whom I'd passed earlier, starting up—tiny black dots against the snow. The sky had cleared, and from the flat, nar-row pass I had tremendous views of the rugged Coast Mountains. North into Canada, somewhere ahead, lay the Yukon.

I knew there was a ranger cabin at the pass, and I had seen a red-clad figure watching me from above as I made the climb, so I wasn't too surprised to be offered a hot drink when I reached ranger Dan's small wooden shelter. As I drank the welcome mug of hot lemonade, Dan, a young and extremely fit looking man from Car-cross not far to the north, explained that the cabin had been built and a ranger stationed there because so many ill-equipped and inexperi-enced hikers attempted the trail and reached the pass suffering from hypothermia. After a hot drink and a rest in the warm cabin (which was hot enough on my visit for Dan to be wearing just shorts and a thin short-sleeved shirt), many people who might otherwise have needed evacuation by helicopter were able to continue, he said. In good weather it was possible to do the whole trail from Dyea to Lake Bennett in a day in lightweight running clothing and with a minimum of gear, as someone had done a few years previously.

As we talked, Matti and Erkki appeared above us on the pass, and I discovered what was in the large plastic bag Erkki carried that seemed a rather odd addition to his otherwise professional and experienced-outdoorsman appearance. It was a camcorder, not by any means the last I was to see on the walk, and he was using it to film Matti walking down to the hut from the pass.

Dan had been expecting us, as Scott at Sheep Camp had radioed to say we were on our way. This careful monitoring of hikers is perhaps necessary on such a popular trail, though it struck me as a little overprotective. I was not too bothered, however, as I knew that in a few days I would have the rest of the summer to wander through much more remote areas where there would be no ranger patrols, no hot drinks and warm huts, and no one who knew exactly where I was. The system wasn't perfect, at any rate; Dan was not aware of the two who had crossed the pass heading south the day before.

Now in Canada, though not yet the Yukon, I descended over extensive snowfields through impressive open alpine scenery above Crater Lake, which was still two-thirds frozen, to the basic and bumpy campsite among scrub trees at Happy Camp, so called because it is the first usable site after Sheep Camp. I was exhilarated by the sense of space, a total contrast to the confined, steep-sided narrow valleys on the Alaskan side of the pass. The weather was still improving, with much sunshine and blue sky, so I continued the fine walk above Long Lake past many small tarns and then through slowly developing woodland to beautiful Deep Lake, where I stopped for a rest. There I was overtaken by Dan, who had finished his shift at the pass and was heading down to the rangers' headquarters at Lake Lindeman. "Another ranger will head up tomorrow," he told me. As we sat by the river he pointed out a mountain goat on the crags nearby, a white billy goat that I could see clearly through my binoculars climbing nimbly over the steep rocks.

The trail continued on beside a deep and impressive canyon, down which meltwater-swollen Moose Creek roared to Lake Lindeman. At the lake, where some of the stampeders built their boats and waited for the ice to break up (others continued down to Lake Bennett, not wanting to risk the rapids between the two lakes), are large campsites and two shelter cabins in the rich lakeside forest. Descending into the forest at Lindeman gives one the feel of having come down from the mountains, but the lake is at an altitude of more than two thousand feet, a thousand feet higher than Sheep Camp.

In one of the shelter cabins I met two German women who had crossed the pass the day before in heavy rain and thick mist. Ironically, they had missed the hut at the summit and the hot drink they so needed. They stopped for the night at Happy Camp, which was windswept and miserable and wet enough to have them cooking in their tent, despite the risk of a bear's visit, since there is no shelter cabin there. As the talk turned to bears, Matti and Erkki arrived. Matti was blasé about the potential danger, saying he had seen lots of grizzlies on previous Alaskan trips and had never had any problems. I felt a little more cautious; I had seen only one grizzly along with several black bears in the wild, and just because no bear had yet caused me problems didn't mean the next one wouldn't. The two Germans were heading to Kluane National Park, where there is a large population of grizzlies; they seemed to lean more toward my way of thinking despite having cooked in their tent the previous night—something I had never done and never intended to do in bear country, though this absolute rule wasn't to last the length of the walk.

With images of ferocious bears drifting through my dreams, the sound of loud splashing in the lake not far from my tent at midnight woke me with a start. I ventured down to the water's edge. In the soft twilight—it never gets truly dark at this time of year this far north—a moose was wading hip deep through the water. On seeing me it veered away and splashed noisily, with a clumsy-looking, high-stepping trot, to the far bank through water up to its neck.

At five I was awakened by the less pleasant sound of heavy

rain drumming on the taut nylon tent. By the time I set off it was torrential, and I welcomed Dan's offer of a cup of coffee at the ranger headquarters, even though I had only been on the trail for five minutes. The previous night twelve people had stayed at Sheep Camp, he told me, and the forecast was for heavy showers and strong winds for at least the next three days. It looked as though I had been lucky enough to cross the pass during the few fine hours in a week of rain. A ranger had set out early in the morning for the hut on the pass, and Dan called her to see what the weather was like higher up. "It's snowing," came the terse reply. Despite the conditions, she was going on to the pass.

The season, said Dan, who had been a ranger on the trail for seven years, had just begun. About two hundred people do the walk in June, but in July and August there can be as many as eighty a day. Then the campgrounds, especially those with shelters, are crowded every night. I was glad to be there in June. All those who complete the trail receive a certificate at Lindeman, and I was given one by Dan. It seemed faintly ironic to be recognized for just the first few days—and almost certainly the easiest and safest period of my walk. I wasn't expecting to find trails remotely resembling the Chilkoot farther north.

After consuming several more cups of coffee I left late in the morning, donning my waterproof rain pants for the first time and carefully zipping my waterproof jacket and snugging the hood against the hammering rain. Above, the clouds were practically brushing the tops of the trees. The trail, muddy and running with water, wandered through rocky terrain above the lake. Across the dark waters the bright glare of fresh snow was visible on the mountains whenever the cloud blanket lifted a little.

At Lake Bennett and the end of the Chilkoot Trail, the sun came out and the clouds rapidly vanished, though they still hung over the mountains around the pass. Lake Bennett is one of the many large lakes, known in the Yukon as the Southern Lakes, that form the headwaters of the Yukon River. On its shores in the late winter and spring of 1898, thousands of people who had come over the Chilkoot and White passes cobbled together boats with handsaws and other tools. The ice broke on May 29, and 7,124 ramshackle vessels carrying some twenty-eight thousand people set off for Dawson City.

The stampeders called it Boat Lake, though to the local Tagish Indians it was Kusooa. The name Bennett was given to it by Lieutenant Frederick Schwatka of the U.S. Army, who led an expedition over the Chilkoot Pass and down the Yukon River in 1883, becoming the first person to navigate the river from end to end. Schwatka named almost everything, usually ignoring any names already in use. Many of his names were later replaced with the earlier ones, but Bennett, named for editor James Gordon Bennett of the *New York Herald,* who was a supporter of American exploration, is one that stuck.

On the slopes overlooking the southern end of the lake stands the wooden St. Andrew's Church, built in 1899 when this was the northern railhead of the White Pass and Yukon Railroad, the existence of which kept a town here long after the other Chilkoot Trail settlements had been abandoned. Today little remains but the empty shell of the church and the boarded-up station. The town died decades ago when the railway was extended to Whitehorse; the railway died in the mid-1980s when the service from Skagway was stopped. Now the trains go no farther than the summit of White Pass. While I regret the closure of a historic and beautiful line, it did give me an easy walk along the old tracks to Carcross. I had considered traversing the mountains above the lake, but the weather forecast and the steep, snow-covered, cliff-lined slopes soaring into the clouds changed my mind.

I sat for a while by the church, looking down the long lake to distant hills. Somewhere along its length I would enter the Yukon. A movement caught my eye, and I spotted Matti and Erkki setting out along the railway tracks. Soon I left the Chilkoot Trail and followed in their footsteps. Judging by the large amount of bear dung, the railway had become a major trail for the local bear population. The walking was easy yet disconcerting, for the ties were just the wrong distance apart for my stride. I stayed on the gravel along the edges when it didn't slope too much for comfortable travel.

After five or so miles I found a beautiful campsite on a little headland between the tracks and the lake. A fire pit and bits of rope tied to trees showed it had been used before, though not recently. There was no sign of bears, only moose tracks on the sandy beach. On this night, my first away from a prepared campground with a shelter cabin, I put into practice the routine I would follow nearly every night for the rest of the summer.

The first step was to locate two sites, one for the kitchen and one for the tent, so that smells from the former wouldn't bring bears to the latter. During the first half of the walk I would also find a tree with branches high and strong enough to hang my food out of reach of bears and other creatures. As I progressed northward the trees grew smaller, until hanging food safely was impossible. Then I simply hid my food in vegetation at least a hundred yards from where I slept. It was all wrapped in foil and plastic in nylon stuff sacks, so the smell was minimal.

The criteria for a good kitchen site were a pleasant view, as this would be where I spent most of my time in camp; a spot where a fire could be lit safely and without leaving any trace unless there was already a fireplace; and if it looked like rain, trees from which I could hang the nylon tarp I had brought as a cooking and eating shelter. A place to sit wasn't a major concern. There was always somewhere. If there wasn't a convenient tree trunk or rock to lean against, I propped my pack up with my staff and used that.

In this camp I had a used fire ring, a log for a backrest, and a spectacular view down the lake, plus a few stout pines nearby for hanging food. Finding a tent site proved more problematic, as would frequently be the case, since it was usually a good spot for the kitchen that first attracted me to a potential site, not a nice flat sleeping area. The headland was small and the areas suitable for a tent were too close to my cooking and food storage area, so I recrossed the tracks and scoured the thicker forest inland for a passable spot. The tent pitched, a procedure that took no more than a few minutes, I laid out my sleeping bag and self-inflating insulating foam mat, zipped the doors against the insects, and returned to the headland. There I tied a rock to a long length of cord, slung it over a high branch, and tied one end around a tree trunk, leaving the other hanging in midair ready for the attachment of my food bag. After scouting the beach to collect driftwood, I was ready to sit down, relax, and have dinner.

Setting up camp took time, especially when I couldn't find a tent site or a branch for the food bag, and I would much rather have cooked and eaten in or just outside the tent in the European fashion. I knew the chances of a bear's raiding camp were slight but still possible, however, so I kept to the safer routine more or less throughout the walk. There are an estimated seven to fifteen thousand black bears and six to seven thousand grizzly bears in the Yukon, which is one of the last strongholds for grizzlies. Bears rarely threaten people unless they get used to eating human foods or garbage. Such spoiled bears can become aggressive and then have to be relocated or destroyed. According to a Yukon Fish and Wildlife pamphlet, *The Bear Facts,* approximately one hundred black bears and fifteen grizzlies have to be destroyed each year because they pose a threat to human safety. Keeping food and garbage away from bears protects them as well as us.

Although the sky remained clear, the sun dropped early behind the ragged, steep-sided ridge towering above the lake, and the temperature dropped with it to a cool forty-six degrees Fahrenheit. The walk's first campfire was welcome. As I watched the shadows lengthen and darken on the calm water I contemplated a high-level route for the next day but made no decision, again leaving it to the weather. Sitting alone by the flickering fire, I felt at peace and as though the walk had really started. The Chilkoot Trail, a fine but overmanaged walk, was behind me. Ahead lay the Yukon and the true wilderness.

I woke to the sound of a gusty wind in the treetops and a chilly touch to the air. The temperature was forty degrees. The mountain-tops were in cloud, and as I breakfasted on cold granola a few spots of rain fell. The railway it was to be. As soon as I set off I encountered fresh bear dung on the tracks, close enough to my camp for the bear to have known I was there.

Near deserted and decaying Pennington Station, its bare rooms littered with old tickets and timetables, I caught a glimpse of something moving in the bushes by the track. It was only a large porcupine. On sensing my presence it immediately turned its back and raised its long spines into a threatening fan. Knowing from previous experience that if I moved to photograph it from the front it would simply keep turning away, I sat down to wait. After a few minutes the animal turned cautiously around. When it realized I was still there it spun away, but not before I got a picture of its face.

Under a dull sky and in a strong cold wind I covered the twenty miles to Carcross at a brisk pace, pausing only at a sign that told me I was entering the Yukon. The boundary may be artificial, but it was symbolic. Here my south-north walk through the Yukon Territory really began, and I felt the journey was truly under way.

I arrived in the tiny hamlet of Carcross to see two large packs propped up outside the only café. Inside, Matti and Erkki were making up for their sparse trail diet, and although I'd had plenty of food, I soon joined them. One rule for long-distance wilderness walking is never to pass by any opportunity for fresh food.

Carcross is an abbreviation of Caribou Crossing, the name the first miners gave this important crossroads where four valleys come together and Tagish-Nares and Bennett lakes meet. Once, vast numbers of caribou migrated twice a year through the narrows. It was a major stopping place on the way to the Klondike and later to the Atlin goldfields in northern British Columbia, and a town sprang up to provide services for the stampeders. By the time the gold rush was over, the town was a halt on the WP&Y railroad, and so it survived. The name was shortened in 1904 due to postal confusion with other places of the same name in the North. Today about 350 people live in Carcross, which is less than an hour's drive from Whitehorse. Tourism is its main business.

The Carcross Community Campground, about half a mile out of town, had no water supply (due to arsenic in the water, according to a local citizen), but the water I fetched from the nearby RV park seemed potable even when Matti and Erkki turned it into Finnish-style coffee over a campfire. As they were scheduled to collect their canoe in Whitehorse in three days, they had decided to walk there on the highway, though Matti was worried about his feet, which were extremely sore, perhaps from walking over rocky terrain in rubber boots. I had more than enough food left for my own trek to Whitehorse, so I donated some to the Finns. I couldn't imagine walking on only twelve hundred calories a day.

"The problem with campgrounds is other people!" So begins my journal entry for the next day, after being awakened at 3:00 A.M. by loud music, raucous shouts, and the over-revved engine of a vehicle roaring at high speed around and around the campground. This racket went on for well over an hour. I arose late, at nine, to find Erkki and Matti, also just up and starting a fire for their morning coffee. It was their custom to stop a couple of times a day to light a fire for coffee. I thought my four or five mugs a day made for a high caffeine intake, but the Finns had five or six times as much coffee in each cup. I was surprised they weren't in Dawson already!

After they left for their road slog I went into Carcross for a café breakfast. It was Sunday, and I was taking the day off, as I wanted to call at the post office next day to send off some exposed film and my first postcards, and hopefully to pick up my first mail from home.

Not wanting another disturbed night, I moved into the rickety Caribou Hotel, which was built in 1898 and is the oldest operating hotel in the Yukon. The Caribou is perhaps most kindly described as having character. It did have a bath and hot water, even if the crumbling plaster was kept out of the water by large sheets of plastic suspended from the ceiling. The price for a room was a very reasonable thirty dollars Canadian. The café and the town's only bar are in the hotel, so all the necessary amenities were at hand.

The main tourist attraction was the SS *Tutshi,* a restored sternwheeler originally launched in Carcross in 1917 and used for luxury cruises on Tagish Lake until 1955. I spent an hour touring the boat and took a few photographs despite the poor light. I'm glad I did, because later in the summer the boat burned in a fire that was apparently started deliberately. For Carcross the loss of the *Tutshi* is a disaster, as most of the bus tours that stopped in the town came to visit the boat.

Lowry Toombs had said he would leave my food at the Visitor Reception Centre beside the *Tutshi,* but it wasn't there. After I phoned Barbara Toombs, who said she would try to contact Lowry, I spent the afternoon writing postcards, waxing my boots, and watching my clothes whiz around in the RV-park laundry. I was just finishing dinner in the café when Lowry walked in, carrying my supplies. "I thought you'd turn up today," he said. "Come and have a beer."

We repaired to the hotel bar just across the corridor. The noisy crowd and smoky atmosphere were a bit of a shock, but the live country music was pleasant, far better than the usual jukebox. Between explaining to various acquaintances of Lowry's what I was doing, I discussed with him my plans for the rest of the trek. He offered much useful advice and said he would try to find me a supply point between Carmacks and Dawson City, the lack of which was my biggest outstanding problem.

"People talking in room next door kept me awake until gone midnight—I nearly packed up and returned to the campground!" The next day's journal entry shows that the move to the hotel was not an unmitigated blessing. Still tired from the previous night's disturbance, I didn't wake until ten. At the post office I collected a postcard of the Snowdonia mountains in Wales and a packet of maps of the Pyrenees, which I was to check for a book I had written. It seemed strange to sit in a Yukon café, poring over maps of the Pyrenees, and I found it difficult to concentrate on the Spanish and French place-names. I spent more time looking at them than at the maps of the route to Whitehorse!

By late morning I was ready to depart on the first true cross-country section of the walk. The Chilkoot Trail had been a false start. So far I had been either on a well-maintained trail or following railway tracks. The next few days would show me whether walking the Yukon was actually feasible, and I left Carcross feeling nervous.

3

The First Peaks

CARCROSS TO WHITEHORSE

JUNE 25–JULY 1, 57 MILES

In wilderness travel it seems that every piece of good luck has to be balanced by an accompanying drawback.

—Dick North, *The Lost Patrol*

North of Carcross lies a roughly triangular-shaped mountain wilderness bordered by the Watson River valley to the west and Tagish and Marsh lakes to the south and east. Much of this area is densely wooded, but a few peaks, outliers of the Coast Range, rise above the trees; the highest are 6,400-foot Caribou Mountain and 6,629-foot Mount Lorne. My hope was to traverse both summits and then descend to Whitehorse. North of Whitehorse I would enter the vast forests of the Yukon Plateau, and it would be a month or more before I would have the chance to venture above timberline again.

The foot of Caribou Mountain lay beyond the Carcross Desert, a strange natural sand pit promoted on a large roadside sign as the world's smallest desert. Its tire-marked pale yellow surface revealed it as a favorite racetrack for off-road vehicles and motorbikes. Beyond the soft sand began the relentless forty-three-hundred-foot climb up the steep, rounded slopes of the mountain. Dense thickets and small trees soon gave way to steep shaley bluffs, then a shattered rocky ridge up which it was quite exciting to scramble, especially with a large, heavy pack. The day was hot and there were many mosquitoes about, forcing me to add insect repellent to the sweat that poured down my face.

Stupidly I had set off with an empty water bottle; my route was up a broad, waterless ridge, and thirst came quickly. By the time the summit slopes approached, finding something to drink was far more important than reaching the top. When I spotted a small patch of white glistening against the turf, I packed my bottle with dirty, grainy old snow, hoping it would melt quickly in the sun. Soon afterward, the rocky terrain gave way to wonderfully soft and cushiony alpine tundra, with a stream running under boulders. Out came the rotten snow stuffed in only minutes before. I filled the bottle with water, gulping it greedily, then donned my windproof jacket against a cool breeze that dried the sweat on my back.

A short final pull capped the five-hour climb to the summit, where I slumped with relief beside the futuristic tall plastic green obelisk that decorated the top. I guessed it might be a weather station but was later told it was a microwave tower; it represented another chapter in the encroachment of technology begun during the gold rush. Whatever its purpose, I was happy to rest against it. The broad and gently sloping summit was strewn with wooden posts, wire, and other junk that suggested a building had been there at one time, perhaps the precursor to the tower.

The view was wide-ranging, with the long dark line of Bennett Lake stretching away to the south amid the serrated snowy ranks of the Coast Range, but it was too cold to linger. Clouds pouring in from the southwest suggested rain, another reason not to dawdle. The effort and time of the ascent led me to seek a campsite not too far from the summit. I headed for a shallow valley with an intermittent stream about two and a half miles away. As I traversed the east slopes of a minor peak to the north of Caribou Mountain, movement high above caught my eye. A caribou cow and calf were delicately high-stepping across the tundra, their gray-brown coats merging with the vegetation and the yellow, lichen-speckled rocks.

A wide, gentle ridge led easily down to the little creek just on the timberline. The thawing snow patches that dotted the hillsides above provided plenty of water. At forty-four-hundred feet this was to be one of the highest camps of the walk. A cold, gusty wind and an evening temperature of forty-eight degrees Fahrenheit made it chilly, so I cleared a patch of gravel and lit a small fire with fallen wood collected from the forest below. But the cool breeze was a welcome mosquito repellent. Whenever it died down for even a few seconds they zoomed in immediately.

By nine the next morning, it was a hot and sticky sixty-two degrees in the tent, though still cloudy outside. The calm air was tense and heavy, with a threat—or perhaps, given its purifying freshness, a promise—of rain. Hordes of mosquitoes forced me to don my windproof jacket despite the heat and spray my hat with bug repellent, a tactic that kept them off my face when I was moving, at least.

Yukon mosquitoes are infamous. Many people I had talked to about the trek asked me how I would cope with the bugs; most reckoned it couldn't be done. I was more worried about mosquitoes than bears, and I arrived in the Yukon with dozens of bottles of a new repellent called Bug Off, donated by a Scottish manufacturer eager to find out how well the stuff worked. I suffered very few bites, and so was able to report that it worked well indeed. Those aromatic green coils that burn like incense were also effective, and I took to lighting one whenever I rested. Overall the Yukon's bugs were not as bad as the midges of home, which may be good news for the Yukon's tourist industry if not for Scotland's!

Moving out, I entered light timber a mile or so beyond my campsite and passed two beaver ponds on the south fork of Lewes Creek before coming upon a faint path in a rich grassy meadow. This soon developed into a good pack trail. Not wishing to pass up such easy hiking, I followed it northwest, hoping it might lead to the confluence of the south fork and Lewes Creek itself. I had abandoned my original aim of striking directly north after a scouting detour to the edge of a wide wooded valley revealed a densely wooded, steep-sided ridge that lay between the south fork and Lewes Creek and looked as though it would be difficult to cross. With a trail as an alternative, I had no inclination to find out just how difficult.

As the morning wore on, the sky darkened and the rain finally fell. After passing a well-used horse camp the trail became a dirt road and veered to the west. The rapidly worsening weather made heading back up above timberline seem unwise, especially as the wet forest was thick and forbidding, so I stayed on the road, which—as I expected—descended to the Watson River valley and the Klondike Highway. As the black pavement came into view the rain intensified and thunder rumbled overhead. I was now several miles west of where I wanted to be, but my map showed a "cart track" heading east-northeast up a creek toward Minto Hill and the Mount Lorne massif. It lay just a couple of miles north along the highway, and I headed for it.

By the time I reached this steep, winding dirt road back up into the hills, the rain was torrential and the thunder deafening and con-stant. With hood up and head down I reascended eight hundred feet of the several thousand I had lost earlier in the day. But the road ended abruptly in a muddy swamp beside a creek, and it was late in the day to commence bushwhacking. Backtracking to an old camp-site I had passed a few minutes earlier, I searched out the site of an old cabin and a decaying outhouse on a bluff above the creek. Cut boughs, a large fire ring on a big square of hard-packed dirt, a crude camp table, fragments of rope, and a dismaying amount of garbage showed the site had been used more recently. I lit a fire of dead wood and burned much of the trash, heaping big logs over the blaze to protect it from the downpour. Slinging a tarp between four large spruces, I sheltered beneath it in front of the fire, lit the stove, and warmed myself with soup and coffee. It looked as though I would be able to light fires frequently, so I made a mental note to buy a lightweight grill in Whitehorse.

The downpour stopped and the sun suddenly appeared halfway through the evening. It was time to survey my surroundings. Not far from camp the forest fell away abruptly into a deep trench, from the lip of which I could look across the wide, green valley of the Watson River, in which lay hidden the White Pass and Yukon Railroad and the Klondike Highway, to the long, steep-sided slopes of Gray's Ridge and farther west and south the distant snowy peaks of the Coast Range. For a long time I gazed out across the forest and mountains, reveling in my wilderness solitude, experiencing the closeness to nature I had come to seek. The walk was becoming my way of life.

Back by the fire I made some calculations. Although I had walked twelve miles in seven hours, my westward deviation had taken me some three miles short of the day's objective and a thousand feet lower. Weather permitting, I might still be able to reach the summit of Mount Lorne the following day. My planned camp had been high above timberline. The shelter of the forest was welcome in the stormy weather.

In the morning the tent was soaked with condensation though the sky was still cloudy. Red squirrels chattered noisily and scrabbled up and down the trees while birds sang farther away. By nine the skies were clearing and I wandered to the edge of the bluff with cameras and tripod. Thick, flowing swirls of white cloud hid the summit of Gray's Ridge and decorated its flanks, an inspiring sight that I watched for an hour or so while my tent, spread over a bush, dried in the sunshine.

There followed, in the words of my journal, "a long 11-hour day, but also one of the best yet and the most enjoyable." It began with a steep climb from the camp back above timberline to a col east of Minto Hill. From this grassy saddle I traversed into a narrow, steep-sided, V-shaped rocky notch whose slopes were mirrored in the tiny pool that lay at its heart. The exquisite symmetrical perfection of the scene held me enthralled. One of the joys of cross-country travel is the discovery of such hidden gems, unmarked on maps, absent from guidebooks. I threaded the boulder-strewn center of the pass to enter a stream system that led, after two and a half hours, to the indistinct col between Bear and Monkey creeks that had been my previous day's intended destination. The walking was easy and the views delightful under a bright sun, the day marred only, and that marginally, by the clouds of mosquitoes that erupted with every footfall.

The long climb of Mount Lorne began with the traverse of grassy bumps, between two of which I found a motorbike. It was so shiny and new it could only have been there a few hours, but I saw no sign of rider or tracks. Perhaps a hunter had used it to gain access to the high hills and was now somewhere close by stalking game, but the bike remained one of those curious finds that often perplex those who wander the hills. I keep a list of such finds, to which I mentally added this, the largest yet.

The steep lower slopes of Mount Lorne soon narrowed to a superb pinnacled rock arête. Several steep and high blocks of rock made scrambling along this crest exciting and difficult. I had to either climb over or delicately balance around them, carefully not looking at the drop below. Several times I thought I would have to retreat, but each time I found a way around the obstacle. This was not really the place for a bulky pack, but my Gregory model at least balanced well. The intense concentration needed to progress safely along this ridge heightened my appreciation of the rock, and I took in every smudge of dark lichen under my hands, every tiny splintering flake of sharp stone. The world narrowed to the next handhold, the next ledge for a boot, and the ridge became a puzzle to be solved, a puzzle I was part of. For a while I experienced the total, exhilarating immersion in the present that is one of the addictive qualities of rock climbing.

From the end of the arête a steep but easy scramble up broad rocky slopes led to a small, neat summit and a magnificent view of the southern Yukon. A great sweep of mountains and lakes lay spread before me. The toy-town block of Whitehorse was visible to the north with the rolling, green wooded hills of the Yukon Plateau beyond it, while far below to the east and south sparkled the long, dark lines of Marsh and Tagish lakes. To the south and west, wave after wave of the Coast Range mountains disappeared into the horizon. It was the immensity, the sheer vastness of the wilderness rather than the details that impressed, and I felt a shiver of excitement and perhaps trepidation as I looked out on what I thought of, for this summer, as my domain. The clearing skies made a brilliant vista, and this was both literally and figuratively the high point of the walk so far. The spectacular view held me for an hour on the summit.

My descent was along another excellent though easier arête, then steeply down loose rocky slopes to a broad saddle. There I diverted west to a small pool I'd picked out on the map as a campsite, but the steep slopes beside it provided nowhere to camp, so I continued on down beside a swelling creek into dense forest and alder thickets in a narrow valley. Just as I was beginning to despair of finding even a small flat spot, I came into a large dry and open area. I'd lost the water but found enough room for several scout troops to camp. I paused to listen for the creek—often the best way to find water—a task made difficult by the whine of mosquitoes. Waving them away and slowly turning from side to side, I detected the faint sound of trickling water, and there was the creek, hidden in a dense alder swamp.

A few cirrus streaks drifted overhead as the sun set and a pale crescent moon came into view. There wasn't a breath of wind. By 11:45 P.M. there was dew on the tent and the temperature was just forty-two degrees Fahrenheit. But I had no need of a fire on this dry evening, and there wasn't, anyway, a place to light one without leaving a scar.

Despite the clear sky, the temperature fell only to thirty-four degrees overnight. By 8:30 A.M. the sun was high and bright in the still, clear sky, and it was already hot. I progressed northward over a series of small, gradually declining, lichen-and-willow-scrub-covered ridges. My aim was to stay above the forest as long as possible, thereby reducing the distance I would have to bushwhack to the Alaska Highway for the last leg to Whitehorse, now only twenty-five miles away.

The morning ended with clouds beginning to cover the sky and a huge black thunderhead towering over the hills to the east. Soon came the first rumbles of the storm, and dark swathes of rain were visible in the distance. The thunder and lightning showed no sign of heading my way, but I was glad not to be on the exposed peak of Mount Lorne with an electric storm in the vacinity.

On the lower crests the brush grew denser, and progress became harder and slower. A large pile of dirt proved to be the residue of an abandoned mine near which I found an old metal claim mark, the first I'd seen, nailed to a tree. A trail headed west, but it soon petered out in a steep, dry, brush-choked valley, so I retreated uphill and, seeking water as well as an easy way to the road, dropped down the other side of the dwindling ridge into a northward-trending valley. It turned out to be a steep-sided, brush-, swamp-, and moss-choked narrow ravine with an intermittent but welcome stream, the first water I'd found since leaving camp. I fought my way down this trench, hoping the small crags that began to loom on either side wouldn't eventually bar my way. The appearance of a passable campsite would have stopped me for the day, but there was none. I kept on, feeling more and more tired, as much in reaction to the previous days' efforts as to the current strenuous bushwhack. Eventually the creek disappeared completely as the valley began to flatten out. In the distance I could just hear the hum of traffic.

Now in open forest, I found and followed a recently maintained trail, picking up speed. Only then did I realize I'd been ambling all day. When the trail turned south, I headed northwest on a compass bearing, trying to maintain a fast pace on the level forest floor. It was surprisingly difficult. My body wanted to move slowly even though my brain wanted to hurry and find a campsite so I could relax completely.

The top of a steep aspen-covered bank gave a clear enough view of the surrounding hills for me to work out approximately where I was in relation to the road, which thankfully was fairly close. I soon happened on another trail that quickly became a dirt road, and then suddenly I was standing on the Alaska Highway, a road I had last seen twenty months earlier at the end of a trek along the Canadian Rockies. Half a mile down the highway the Sourdough Country Campsite appeared. It was 9:15 P.M. Arriving hot, sweat-soaked, and extremely thirsty, I was quite happy to pay eighteen dollars for a site and a shower and two dollars for two cans of Pepsi.

The roadside campground had spacious dusty pitches under big spruce trees, most occupied by giant RVs. I felt out of place but relieved to be there. I had nearly stopped on several occasions at woefully unsuitable places in the forest, but now I was glad I had kept going despite growing fatigue. During my ten o'clock supper of multibean soup laced with margarine and curry powder, I studied the map. I had covered twelve miles in a straight line but had probably walked half again as much. But now it was just a highway plod into Whitehorse.

When I considered the four days' walk from Carcross (Only four days! It felt much, much longer.), I felt as though I had passed a test of my own devising. On this first cross-country venture I had walked forty-four miles, an average of eleven a day and close enough to my aim of twelve, climbed two mountains, and had a first taste of bushwhacking. It was hard and I was tired, but more important, it had been fun. I knew, too, that as the days and weeks went by I would grow stronger.

Despite the unfamiliar traffic noise, I slept well until the heat of the morning awakened me. A refreshing shower was followed by breakfast in the gas station café at Carcross Corner, a mile down the road. The heaped stack of hotcakes doused in maple syrup made a welcome change from cold granola. Then came the long highway walk, the only distraction from the heat, noise, and diesel fumes being the colorful billboards advertising Whitehorse attractions.

The Alaska Highway is probably one of the most famous roads in the world. It was built in 1942–43 during the Second World War by U.S. Army engineers so that supplies could be delivered overland to Alaska, which was potentially vulnerable to a Japanese invasion. It cost $140 million, an enormous sum in the 1940s. The first automobile road to Alaska, it was opened to the public in 1946. Running 1,360 miles from Dawson Creek in British Columbia to Fairbanks, Alaska, the Alaska Highway is the main route through the southern Yukon. *The Milepost,* an annual guide to the highway and other northern roads, lists roadside attractions by their distance from Dawson Creek; many businesses advertise using their mileage number even though distances in Canada are now given in kilometers.

As I neared the capital I left the highway to visit Miles Canyon and Schwatka Lake on the Yukon River. The canyon and the Whitehorse Rapids at its head were the main obstacles to the Klondikers sweeping downstream toward Dawson. After a few initial disasters, the Mounties made sure the stampeders unloaded and portaged their goods around the rapids while their boats were taken through by professional pilots or pulled through on ropes. Now the lake, created by a dam built in 1959, has killed the whitewater that gave the city its name (the early miners thought the rapids looked like the manes of white horses), and cruise boats laden with tourists ply the waters while float planes line the banks.

Whitehorse became the capital of the Yukon in 1951, usurping the title from Dawson City. The coming of paved highways to the territory, particularly the Alaska Highway, which skirts the edge of Whitehorse and then turns west for Alaska, left Dawson isolated far to the north. The Whitehorse Rapids were so called by 1887, and the flat land at the foot was an obvious stop-off point for the stampeders. The town site was surveyed in 1899, and a permanent settlement began the following year.

At the southern end of Whitehorse on the west bank of the Yukon lies the Robert Service Campground, a site reserved for tent campers. I headed into it, keen to dump my gear before going into town. The campground was pleasant and the price reasonable, but the pitches, sand over gravel pads, were awful. It was almost impossible to get my stakes to hold in the soft, shifting ground. A free-standing dome tent would have been fine, but my lightweight single-hoop model required a minimum of nine stakes to stand.

I had spent more than enough time touring Whitehorse on my earlier visit. My concern was to sort supplies and head back out as quickly as possible, so I dumped my gear in the tent and walked into town to collect mail and see if the missing food box had arrived. It had, along with a sixty-dollar customs bill Yukon Tourism had paid.

Because Sunday would be Canada Day and Monday a public holiday, Saturday became a day of chores. I spent the morning writing letters, and shopping for small pieces of gear I thought would make life in the bush easier. At Hougen's Sports Lodge I found a filter funnel in case I could only buy dubious fuel for the stove in the months ahead, a liter of nice, clean Coleman fuel, a mosquito coil holder, and a lightweight campfire grill. I hoped the extra weight of the grill would be canceled by the need to carry less stove fuel.

At midday I met George Sinfield and went to his house to re-sort the supplies I'd left behind, adding the stuff that had just arrived. I seemed to have ordered vast amounts of broccoli soup! George's back porch took on the appearance of a supermarket stockroom as I spread heaps of supplies over the floor and sat among them trying to make order out of chaos. To add to the confusion, I was throwing coffee, sugar, toilet paper, and paperback books along with the dinners into those boxes that were going to resupply points without towns or stores. "Should be about right," I wrote hopefully in my journal when I'd finished.

Before sealing and labeling the boxes, I had to make some final decisions about supply points and route, as I wouldn't see these boxes again until I needed them. My problems were greatly eased by George, who generously offered to deliver supplies to

Carmacks and Dawson City himself and to sort out the delivery and caching of the ones to be dropped along the Dempster Highway farther north. A company that ran bus tours along the highway would probably be willing to handle that task, he said.

We discussed possible drop points along the Yukon River between Carmacks and Dawson City. Food caches were essential if I was to walk Gus Karpes's suggested route, which would take about three weeks. The problem was how to put them out, and we didn't come up with any ideas.

Richard Mostyn, a reporter for the *Yukon News*, had interviewed me before I left Whitehorse for the start of the walk, and George gave me a clipping of the feature, which had appeared on June 20, the day I took shelter from the storm in the Sheep Camp cabin on the Chilkoot Trail. My obsession with the missing food box was evident, as my opinions on parcel couriers appeared several times! Tucking the piece into my notebook, I little realized how often it would be mentioned by people I met in the months to come. I hadn't yet really begun to understand that despite its size the Yukon, by virtue of its sparse population, functions socially like a small town. And in a small town everybody reads the local paper.

Later in the afternoon, fed up with piles of soup packets and stacks of maps, George and I drove out to the cabin Gus Karpes had built on the shores of Lake Laberge, a lake immortalized by Robert Service in, "The Cremation of Sam McGee":

> There are strange things done in the midnight sun
> By the men who moil for gold;
> The Arctic trails have their secret tales
> That would make your blood run cold;
> The Northern Lights have seen queer sights,
> But the queerest they ever did see
> Was that night on the marge of Lake Lebarge,
> I cremated Sam McGee.

* * *

After a few beers with Gus we drove on to Takhini Hot Springs, discovered in 1907, where there is a campground and restaurant. The mineral springs today bubble up into a fenced-in concrete swimming pool and have lost all semblance of a natural wonder. They were my destination by foot in two days' time. From the springs we continued along the valley of the Takhini (the name comes from the Tagish Indian *Tahk-Heena,* which means "Mosquito River") down an increasingly bumpy and muddy dirt road. Our goal was to locate the start of the long-abandoned Dawson Road, which I meant to follow at least partway to Carmacks. The Dawson Road was a winter route used by horse-drawn wagons as an alternative to the frozen rivers and once had a series of roadhouses providing food and accommodation. Although it is still marked on the maps, most people I talked to reckoned it would be hard to find on the ground. We certainly couldn't find it from the car, but I was to learn later we were driving on it!

Driving back to Whitehorse, it occurred to me I should have dropped my food supplies at the Takhini hot springs, saving twenty-five pounds on the first day's twenty-mile hike. "No problem," said George. "I'll bring it out on Monday. I need to see the owner of the springs anyway about some horses for a promotional photo shoot for Tourism."

That evening I had dinner with George and Gus. My abrupt return to civilization had left me somewhat bewildered, a state of mind recognized by Gus. "I know how you feel," he said, with a smile that told me he did. For fifteen years he had led wilderness trips, and he talked of how the wilderness affects people. Some, he said in his laconic way, couldn't cope with the solitude even when part of a group, and many marriages ended in divorce as couples who had rarely spent more than a few hours a day together discovered they couldn't stand each other twenty-four hours a day in the bush. Gus no longer leads river trips, preferring to enjoy the river by himself. Although born in Holland, he is a committed Yukoner.

Back at the campground I tried to read a newspaper, but was

too tired. I looked at my watch. It was twenty-five minutes past midnight. For the first time it really sank in just how much daylight there is so far north at that time of year.

Next morning West Germany was beating Czechoslovakia 1–0 in World Cup soccer on the café television. The live broadcast could have been coming from another planet. I finished breakfast just in time to see the tail end of the Canada Day parade pass by. George's little dog Brew brought up the rear, frantically barking at the horses. "He loves parades," George said. We followed the crowds down to the park opposite the SS *Klondike*, where country music boomed from a stage and concession booths dotted the grass. Groups of people wandered desultorily or sat on the ground watching passersby and staring at the blue sky. It was all reminiscent of a summer fete in a small English country town.

At the SS *Klondike* we met Red Grossinger, resplendent in his Canadian Legion uniform. The badges on his beret told of his tours of duty with the United Nations peace-keeping force in Cyprus. He knew George well, and he remembered me from my excursion on his *Youcon Kat* two weeks earlier. The meeting proved fortuitous: Red was piloting a tour group downriver to Dawson in two weeks and agreed to drop supplies for me at Fort Selkirk, an abandoned settlement on the west bank that was being restored by the local Indian band, and at Stewart Island at the mouth of the Stewart River, where there was a homestead. "You'll have to light a fire so they can come and fetch you by boat," he told me.

Red doubted I'd be able to cross either the White or the Sixty-Mile River on foot; I'd need to hitch rides on passing boats. Neither did he think there was much of a trail beyond Fort Selkirk. But at least my longest section—from Carmacks to Dawson—was now broken into three, which made it look far more feasible, problems with fords notwithstanding. I could now label my boxes, splitting one of them for two drops between Carmacks and Dawson. The final decision on a route beyond Fort Selkirk would have to wait until I was there.

A ceremony was held in front of the SS *Klondike* to naturalize new citizens of Canada. It was simultaneously formal and informal, serious and light-hearted, and strangely moving and powerful to someone who'd never had to swear allegiance to any country. I realized I had no idea how people became citizens of Britain.

With two weeks or more of trail food looming in the future, I dined on a huge and superb pizza at Christie's Downtown Place. My appetite was already growing: I had abandoned half-finished a pizza the same size before the walk started.

Rain began to fall as I strolled the short, now familiar route back to the campground, but as soon as I slung the tarp over the picnic table, the sun came out. A fire lit from the ample supplies of wood ready-cut for campers soon had water boiling for coffee. As I gulped the first hot mouthful, Bill, the campground warden, stopped by. "There's a guy on that site over there you should talk to," he said. "He's a photographer too."

The young, dark-haired man sitting outside a small tent turned out to be an aspiring travel and outdoor photographer from Toronto who was spending a couple of months in the Yukon. Alan Sirulnikoff had already been to Dawson and enthused about the light there. "I'm considering hiking the Chilkoot," he said, giving me an opportunity to enthuse in turn. He was traveling mostly by vehicle and had a full bag of camera gear that made me feel underequipped. I particularly envied his fast telephoto lens and heavyweight tripod. I wouldn't want to carry them far, however, and I wasn't surprised to learn he intended taking just one camera body and two lenses on the Chilkoot Trail. After an evening of entertaining talk, we both took photographs of the red, midnight sunset over the river—not that it ever gets fully dark this far north in early July; the sun only vanishes for a few hours.

I am the land that listens, I am the
land that broods;
Steeped in eternal beauty, crystalline
waters and woods.
—Robert Service, "The Law
of the Yukon"

4

Vanished Roads: In Search of the Dawson and Dalton Trails

The saying "Red sky at night, sailor's delight," implying fine weather after a colorful sunset, didn't work in the Yukon, at least on the occasion of my departure from Whitehorse. I woke to torrential rain. By the time I set off it had eased to a mere downpour, but I lingered over a large breakfast in the Edgeware Hotel before starting the long walk out of town. The traffic was a little heavy for comfort, and the rain had cleared to a hot, dry day. I wore running shoes and carried the boots. The twenty miles to the Takhini Hot Springs campground passed slowly. I read much of the way as I walked. It was not an enjoyable day.

At the Hot Springs I set up my tent on the crowded campground, then collected the food supplies George had dropped off just a few hours earlier. Somehow we'd missed each other on the road. The boxes felt like lead weights as I lugged them back to my camp. When I sorted through them I found thirteen days' food, which seemed a little excessive. Had it only been two days ago I'd packed my supplies? Supper was a snack in the Hot Springs café surrounded by the glowing bodies of bathers. Afterward I strolled down to the placid Takhini River to watch a gentle sunset turn the gathering clouds pink.

I set out next day on a good gravel road headed west beside the river. The road narrowed and deteriorated as I left the few farms behind. Across the wide, slow, murky Takhini River I could see traffic on the Alaska Highway. The day started calm and sunny with a little high cloud, yielding by midafternoon to a warm west wind and massive thunderheads in the south. This time the rain passed me by.

After twelve miles, enough for the first day out with the heaviest load of the walk so far, I camped in a pleasant, open aspen wood. During the evening the wind dropped and the sky began to clear. Tiny gray moths fluttered everywhere, getting themselves stuck on my freshly waxed boots and tangled in the tent's insect netting. The evening was warm and I didn't bother lighting a fire.

By noon the next day I'd reached the junction with the Dawson Trail, a clear dirt road at this point. Distant hills lay to the south and west, while to the north, ahead, lay the Miners Range, the last outliers of the Coast Mountains. Beyond them the hills dwindled into the rolling forested uplands of the Yukon Plateau. The sense of space, of endless wilderness, of land untrammeled and free surpassed anything I had yet experienced on the trek; I would encounter it again and again, and it became for me the essence of the Yukon. I felt at last as though I were leaving civilization behind not just for a few hours or days but for as long as I wanted. After sixteen days, the walk was finally beginning to have a meaning, an overall completeness.

The Dawson Trail turned north up the broad Little River valley. Snowshoe hares in summer brown darted from the dense grass, startled out of their daytime snoozing. After a mile or so the track split. As would happen many times in the weeks to come, I had to guess which of two trails—neither marked on the map and both heading roughly in the direction I wanted to go—was the right one. And not for the last time I made the wrong decision. Or rather several wrong decisions. I began with the right fork but soon decided it was veering too far east and retraced my steps. The left fork set off confidently into the trees only to dead-end abruptly in dense brush. I returned to the right-hand track. Shortly after the point where I had turned back the first time, it turned into a good pack trail that headed northeast to a ford of a fast, ankle-deep creek. There I lost the trail in an area of muskeg swamp and beaver ponds, beyond which I found a confusing network of horse trails heading in all directions. The tinkling of bells indicated a number of horses grazing nearby.

I headed for the bank of the Little River, which the map showed the Dawson Trail crossing thereabouts, to be confronted by a murky, swollen stream with steep banks and, as I found by sounding it with my staff, a deep muddy bottom that I didn't fancy disappearing into. I wove my way northward through an old burned area parallel to the river, walking much of the way on the banks of a dry creek bed sprinkled with small oxbow ponds. Thunder rumbled in the afternoon and I caught the edge of the storm, sheltering under a bush when a strong wind brought heavy rain and a little hail. The valley bottom was wet and brush-choked, and I had to head away from the river to find a dryish campsite in a stand of black spruce where the land began to slope up into the Miners Range.

Open potentilla-dotted flats, dense alder thickets, muskeg swamps, and interlaced mats of deadfall impeded the next day's progress up the valley. The Dawson Trail was marked on the map as crossing a low divide into the next valley to the west, so if I hoped to find it I had to ford the river. After approaching and retreating from the muddy stream a few times I finally found a spot where the bed was firm and stony enough for a knee-deep ford. My boots were already wet from sloshing through the swamps, so there was no need to remove them. A further ford of a crotch-deep oxbow pond as I bushwhacked away from the river kept them that way.

Beyond the pond was a large area of cleared ground strewn

with rusting machinery and large fuel cans, the site of Little River, an abandoned homestead. The machinery was old and overgrown, but there were signs that the site had been visited more recently. On one still silvery can I could read the words *sans sucre, avec aspartame.* What is it that ensures, once a place is marked by humans, that future passersby will feel obliged to add their mark? Certainly garbage attracts garbage, as I was to see frequently throughout the walk. Strange, too, is the process, which I first saw on the Chilkoot Trail, that transforms unsightly litter over time into interesting historical artifacts. The decaying farm implements had character and spoke of a vain attempt to wrest a living from the wilderness. Looking at them, I wondered who had lived there, where they had come from, and why they had left. The more modern detritus merely annoyed and saddened me that people would sully what they had come to see.

A good pack trail led away from the site. From the fairly fresh look of the cut deadfall, I judged it had been cleared within the last year, probably by the trappers who had left their rusty traps hanging from trees along the way. The trail climbed out of the valley to follow a sandy ridge into lodgepole pine forest and then plunge into dense alders before emerging suddenly onto the shores of a most beautiful lake glinting in the sunlight. Here was magic indeed. The surprise view was a delight and I floated effortlessly along the lake's narrow sandy shore, following myriad horse prints. Fatigue and strain left me. My body still plodded along, step after step, the heavy pack pressing down, but my mind was free, dancing beside the lake, absorbed in its overwhelming perfection.

The lake was about half a mile long and a quarter-mile wide, its edge bright green with reeds. Beyond the strip of sandy beach were low forested hills, and beyond them the bare undulating peaks of the Miners Range to the east and the Sifton Range to the west. I stopped by the outlet creek. I'd known from the instant I saw the lake that I would camp on its shores. The beach made an ideal site. I leaned my pack against the bank as a backrest and sat down to gaze at the quiet water. Across the lake was 6,739-foot Pilot Mountain, the highest in the Miners Range. The peak was used as a landmark by the first riverboat pilots on the Yukon River, hence the name. Martins swooped over the water in search of insects, dark clusters of ducks moved slowly far out from the bank, sandpipers bobbed and dipped along the shore, a golden eagle sailed slowly overhead to perch in a tree on the far side. One of the ducks moved close inshore, its thin white neck ring, dark brown head, and bright eye identifying it as a goldeneye.

After a while a faint stirring of hunger propelled me to begin setting up camp. Pegs won't hold in sand, so I looked for a tent site away from the beach. In the alders just behind my rest spot I found an old campsite with a fire ring containing several half-burned logs. Empty whiskey bottles, plastic bags, food packets, and cans were scattered nearby. The calming atmosphere of the place was such that for once I wasn't upset by this garbage, sadly typical of a hunters' camp and showing that for some people the lack of wilderness stewardship that characterized the gold miners is still the norm. Beyond this mess the outlet creek faded into the shrunken remnants of another, smaller lake, now mostly a wet meadow. A small sheltered patch of grass in the alders at its edge proved just big enough for the tent.

I gathered all the burnable garbage and carried it back to the beach, where I lit a large fire on the sand below the high-water mark. Firewood was plentiful, as bundles of driftwood lined the lake's edge. Once the initial smoky blaze of rubbish had died down, I set my new grill over the fire. On it I placed the pan and mug, both filled with water from the outlet creek. Slicing open a foil pack of freeze-dried pasta and sauce, I watched as the yellow flames licked around the base of my pan, slowly blackening and dulling the silver sheen of the steel. Soon wisps of steam drifted under the lid, tentatively at first, then more urgently. I plucked the pan from the flames with a bandanna-wrapped hand, then tipped the meal into the boiling water, gave it a quick stir, replaced the lid, and set it aside for ten minutes to rehydrate. By this time the water in the mug was bubbling furiously and I removed that too from the grill, spooned in some instant coffee and sugar, and waited for it to cool a little before adding dried milk. By the time I'd drunk my coffee, the meal was ready. I leaned back against my pack, the pan balanced on a map on my lap, and ate slowly, staring over the lake. I was at one with the world. This was what I had come for.

The evening had been calm and mild, with high drifting clouds and hazy, gentle sunlight. At nine, without warning, there was an abrupt change. Suddenly it was very windy, and dense black clouds rushed across the sky. For several minutes large spots of rain fell and I prepared to retreat into the trees. Then, as quickly as it had appeared, the storm passed. Half an hour later the sky was clear.

Across the lake Pilot Mountain looked on fire, the clouds behind it burning a dull red in the late evening sunlight. At one corner a smudge of rainbow curved up into the sky. The light became extraordinary as the rainbow grew brighter and larger against the dark red clouds and was reflected in the lake. The display intensified as the storm passed over the peak, then slowly faded as the clouds drifted northward, trailing a ragged gray hem in their wake and leaving behind a calm and austere pale blue sky. I shook myself and stood, surprised to find my clothes damp with dew.

Hot sun woke me early, though the overnight low had been thirty-eight degrees. The tent was dripping with condensation. I breakfasted on the beach as the lake shimmered in the sunlight. I was reluctant to leave but knew that I must. There was much to look forward to, though. For the next twelve miles the trail wound through the Klusha Creek valley past a string of lakes, all, like this one, just below timberline at around twenty-nine hundred feet and possibly just as magical.

On the far side of the wet meadow the trail widened into a dusty jeep track that made for easy walking. The dry spruce-pine forest was interspersed with occasional meadows and marshes. Every so often the trees would open to reveal another beautiful lake, the water always wonderfully clear. As I rested by one of them, two handsome common loons swam and dived in front of me. At another I watched a beaver swim by and a bald eagle drift over the water. Red-winged blackbirds, magpies, and gray jays called from the forest and flitted across the meadows. Dragonflies darted in and out of the reed beds, while in the meadows butterflies slipped from flower to flower. Biting insects were rare. At one point I came across the fresh paw prints of a grizzly bear on the trail. In places just the claw marks were visible in the hard earth.

Signs that this was once a regularly traveled trail still remain, most of them impersonal artifacts but a few providing a link with the individuals who once came this way. In one place a square of neat wooden fencing not far off the track marked the grave of a pet dog. On the wooden cross above it was carved the following epitaph:

In Loving Memory
of
Dooley
The Pet Dog
of Mr & Mrs E. Barwash
Died Aug 28th 1918
Aged 4 Years 6 Months

Modern use of the trail was evident by the traps decorating trees along the way, many with grisly skeletons still hanging from them, plus a few hunters' or trappers' campsites, usually with attendant litter. The worst of these kept me from camping by the last lake, lovely though it was. On a bluff overlooking the lake I found a scene of total squalor. Piles of rubbish littered the ground around several ruined cabins, their windows broken and doors hanging open. A magazine dated 1988 showed the camp, presumably an outfitter's operation, had only been abandoned a few years before. Recently used fire rings suggested people still camped nearby. I could have done the same, but the place sickened me so much I wanted it out of my sight even if I had to walk half the night to find another spot. I couldn't comprehend the mentality of those who could desecrate such beauty. Although only a few people venture into the Yukon backcountry, it was becoming clear that most of those who did were in search of game or gold, not wilderness. The "leave no trace" ethos of the modern backpacker has not yet reached the Yukon despite the advice given in the excellent *Wilderness Travelers' "No Trace" Checklist,* a leaflet published by Yukon Renewable Resources that I'd picked up in Whitehorse. The leaflet was subtitled *How to Keep Others from Knowing You Were There!* If only . . .

I marched on grimly, energized by burning anger but troubled by a lurking contradiction. The paths that were easing my passage through the wilderness were made by the same people who left the garbage I so resented.

Another hour's walking in dense forest took me to a good campsite on a grassy bluff forty feet above Klusha Creek. A half rainbow was a faint reminder of the glories of the previous night, but my attention was on the more prosaic matter of a route for the next few days. The track I was following continued along Klusha Creek to join the Klondike Highway some forty-two miles from Carmacks. The alternative was to head west into the Nordenskiöld River valley and follow that until it too reached the highway, eighteen miles closer to Carmacks. No trails were marked on the map following this route. The choice would be between difficult, not to say desperate, bushwhacking in the wilderness or easy walking on a paved road.

I fell asleep without deciding what to do, though the taste I'd had of bushwhacking in the river valleys of the Yukon Plateau inclined me toward the road. Later a noise outside the tent woke me, and I peered out cautiously. Twenty feet away a large red fox, all russet and black, stared at me for a few brief seconds before loping quietly off into the forest. It was one of those fleeting moments of close contact with a wild animal that can occur when you're alone in the wild, but afterward I remembered that my food bags were lying on the ground under a bush a hundred yards away, as I'd been unable to find branches high or strong enough to support them. I fell back to sleep hoping they would be intact come morning.

I needn't have worried. Foxes are probably not interested in freeze-dried food anyway.

The track continued through dense scrub-covered meadows and occasional thickets of trees, crossing the creek at a place marked "Kynocks (site)" on the map. There was nothing there, not even the remains of a bridge. The ford was just deep enough to soak my feet. Fungi grew everywhere: large shiny brown toadstools, pale gray ones emerging from horse dung, little bright red ones half hidden in the grass, and many more. The valley gradually broadened and began to curve to the northeast. The hills faded away into long low wooded ridges, one of which ended abruptly in a prominent fire-red nose of rock.

Before I reached this landmark the track joined another, more frequently used trail, not marked on my maps. One fork headed southeast, away from the road. My decision was made. Not to follow such a track would have been to abandon any sense of adventure. The track went back across Klusha Creek just below a beaver pond that was almost large enough to be called a lake. The overflow from the dam flooded the track, and I had to wade through knee-deep water for a hundred yards. At times I could look up a few feet to the waters of the large pond, held back by the dense latticework of trees and branches, impressive evidence of the beaver's engineering skills.

Finding this unexpected trail changed my mood completely. I had not been looking forward to what seemed only minutes earlier an inevitable long road slog. I didn't know where or how far this track went, but I didn't mind. Indeed, I looked forward to finding out, and my pace picked up. "The predictable has suddenly become the unknown," I wrote in my journal that afternoon. Ahead, the long steep-sided ridge of Mount Vowles came into view on the far side of the Nordenskiöld River.

From the beaver dam the track went over a low pass on the divide separating the Klusha Creek and Nordenskiöld River valleys. High up on the north side of the pass were superb views of both valleys winding away southward to distant hills. On either side rose Cub Mountain and Division Mountain, which, despite their names, were gentle wooded hills under four thousand feet. I was learning that on the Yukon Plateau the word mountain does not mean what it does elsewhere.

The track dropped down along the edge of a steep bluff toward a small lake fringed with reed beds. But just before it reached the lake, it turned ominously to the south and almost immediately crossed the small creek that drained the little tarns in the heart of the pass. On the far side of this creek was a flat open area dotted with small aspens and willows that looked like a good campsite. Old fire pits, decaying cut wood green with moss, and a few rusty tin cans showed others had thought so, too.

There I stopped. I had walked thirteen and a half miles—not a long day, but with the track turning south and my route lying north, the next thirty or so miles might be all bushwhacking. Evening was neither the time to start a difficult route nor the time to pass a good camp. I excavated the charcoal of a fire pit and gathered twigs. A bush gave shelter from the strong wind that had sprung up. I set up the tent back in the shrubbery while several noisy magpies flew around the camp and cackled at me from nearby trees.

That evening I made my first cooking error. "Add 4 ½ cups of water," said the packet labeled Pasta Roma, meaning two cups, not, as I had understood it, four and a half cups. The result was a very soupy but still tasty meal. Probably I needed the liquid. Then I attended to other chores, rinsing out dirty socks and replacing the broken shockcord on my waterproof nylon pack cover with nylon parachute cord. It took a while to carefully thread a needle tied to the cord through the long closed channel around the edge of the cover. I also patched a few large tears, though I noted in my journal: "Really, this cover is shot, pinholes everywhere."

Half an hour before midnight I went for a stroll to confirm that the track did indeed go the wrong way. After following it to where it forded the river, there black with mud, I climbed a steep slope to a hilltop from where I could see it continuing south down the valley. To the north there was no sign of a trail, but a grassy shelf running along the edge of some wooded bluffs above the river looked as though it might provide easy walking for a short way at least. I had come too far to think of turning back, even if all I had to look forward to was difficult bushwhacking.

Although there were no trails on the ground or marked on the maps, I still hoped to find traces of the old Dalton Trail that once ran up the Nordenskiöld valley en route to the Klondike. This had been a Chilkat Indian trade route between the coast and the interior. Then in 1891 Jack Dalton, a famous Yukon and Alaska pioneer who had explored the region the previous year on the *Frank Leslie Illustrated Newspaper* expedition, brought horses into the Yukon for the first time and began building trading posts and a toll road along the route all the way from the Lynn Canal to Fort Selkirk on the Upper Yukon River. It was the only route to the goldfields over which livestock could be easily driven and quickly became important. In the winter of 1897–98 the American government sent a herd of 539 reindeer, imported with their Lapp herders from Scandinavia, along it to relieve the famine that was reported in the Klondike. Only a fifth of the herd survived the journey, and they arrived long after the end of the food shortage, which wasn't in fact very serious. A railway was once planned for the route, but the idea was dropped after the White Pass and Yukon Railroad was started. As the railroad and riverboat traffic increased, the trail fell into disuse.

Other names reflect the history of the area, albeit more indirectly. The Nordenskiöld River was named in 1883 by Frederick Schwatka during his U.S. Army expedition down the Yukon River, after Swedish Arctic explorer Baron Adolf Eric Nordenskiöld who in 1878–79 had made the first journey through the Northeast Passage. The point where the Nordenskiöld flows into the Yukon was called Thuch-en-Dituh, "the Meeting Place," by the Indians, as it was where the interior Indians and the Chilkats met every year to trade. The main landmark in the northern Nordenskiöld River valley, 5,151-foot Mount Vowles (incorrectly given as Vowel Mountain on the 1:50,000 map), was named in 1910 after Royal North West Mounted Police officer Stanley Vowles, who worked in the area.

The harsh screech of a magpie woke me the next morning. Across the river the craggy slopes of Mount Vowles glowed red and fiery in the low, slanting sunlight. The flat-bottomed valley was a tangle of ponds, oxbow lakes, marshes, reed beds, winding creeks, alder and willow thickets, stands of dense spruce, and webs of deadfall. It took me eight exhausting hours to progress eight miles down the valley, though I walked far more than that distance. As far as possible I stayed just above the valley floor on the open grassy slopes of the bluffs, but in many places these faded away into dense forest and I was forced down into the jungle below. Game trails helped at times, as did stretches of dry grassy meadows, but there weren't many of these. At one point I had to negotiate steep brush-choked slopes on the west side of an isolated hummock ringed by red cliffs, and my progress dwindled to almost nothing. I was making too much noise to see any wildlife, but four ravens on a rock outcrop gave away the location of a dead lynx, barely more than skin and bones but stretched out with its teeth bared as if it had died running.

Camp that night was on a dry bluff about twenty-five feet above the marshy valley bottom and gave a good view across to Mount Vowles. A gentle breeze kept off the bugs that had plagued me during the day. Beaver splashed in the ponds below as I sat reading Jack London's *Call of the Wild*. I had just reached the end, when Buck responds to the call and joins the wolves, when a mournful howling began across the valley. This first wolf chorus of the trek was brief, but it enhanced the valley's solitude and wildness immeasurably.

I woke to the steady hum of mosquitoes and the more pleasant chattering of squirrels and songs of birds, backed by the gentle ripple of the river. A gray sky threatened rain, though the clouds were thin. Difficult swampy terrain with too much brush and deadfall soon gave way to easy walking in open flower meadows, beyond which lay spruce forest and more marshes. The best walking terrain was on the narrow margin between the forest proper and the willows and alders that fringed the marshes and ponds. As I picked my way through the bush, large noisy deerflies buzzed around my head. The near absence of mosquitoes due to the breeze was welcome, though. As the day progressed, spots of rain started to fall; by late afternoon they had coalesced into a steady drizzle. It was difficult to work out exactly where I was because I spent so much time zigzagging around obstacles, and there were few obvious landmarks. Two wooded hummocks visible from the shore of a lake finally pinpointed my position early in the evening. A side creek half a mile farther on would be my destination for the day. I pushed on in the continuing drizzle.

I heard Schwatka Creek before I saw it—it lay in a steep-sided, bush-rimmed dark channel deep in the forest. I made camp fifty yards from the south bank, erecting the tarp between two large spruces next to a cluster of fallen trees. The temperature was fifty-four degrees Fahrenheit, but the rain and damp made it feel much colder, so I cleared a patch of spruce needles to reach bare soil and lit a small fire at the mouth of the tarp. The bright warmth had a powerful effect. Suddenly my little shelter became friendly and cozy. I felt a sharp distinction between the enclosed space under the tarp and the world beyond. "Outside," the rain continued steadily and all was dark and wet, the forest threatening and forbidding. "Inside," snuggled into my fleece jacket in front of the fire, I felt as secure and content as if I were at home—so relaxed, in fact, that I was reluctant to leave the tarp and retire to the tent. I could have stared into the fire all night, convinced that in the flickering orange flames lay secrets about to be revealed. It was a satisfying end to a long hard day and a camp that, despite the viewless surroundings and the wet, dull weather, became one of the most memorable of the walk.

The tent was soaked with condensation the next morning; even parts of the inner were very wet. The temperature was a miserably damp thirty-eight degrees and I felt chilly enough, even in my knitted hat, fleece top, and rain jacket, to relight the fire, the first time I'd done so in the morning. But over breakfast I noticed that above the trees the sky had blue patches and the clouds were white, not gray. Shafts of sunlight gave color to tree trunks and patches of forest floor. It began to feel drier and a gusty breeze swirled the smoke around. The forest seemed friendlier and less gloomy as I set off.

It was my ninth day out of Whitehorse, and I hoped to reach Carmacks in three days. My supplies of lemonade powder, coffee, and granola bars were running low, and I was completely out of toilet paper (Jack London had to do instead!). I did have more than enough freeze-dried meals left, so I was unlikely to go hungry.

Fresh bear droppings within ten minutes of camp made an exciting start to the day. I hadn't hung my food either. A few minutes later I found a large spruce bridging the Nordenskiöld River. On the far side I could see saw marks on the stump. Hoping to find a trail, I crossed the log, stepping carefully around the spiky branches. When no trail showed itself, I struck away from the river in search of one as heavy rain began to fall. To my delight, within three-quarters of an hour I came across a good, well-blazed, and recently maintained trail on a shelf well above the river. It led to a new cabin, constructed of large chipboard panels rather than logs, then across an area of deadfall to a huge marsh into which it plunged. I did the same. An awkward wade across wet tussocks to a tree "island" ensued, followed by more paddling. The marsh was fringed with dense brush and deadfall, so it seemed the easiest route, if rather unpleasant.

Unsurprisingly, somewhere in the marsh I lost the line of the trail. In a series of dry or semidry oxbow meadows I found occasional signs of it along with a little too much bear dung. I cast around for a bit, then picked one from a network of jeep tracks that appeared close to the river and followed it west and up in the hope that it might turn northward and parallel the road to Carmacks. Although long disused except by bears and occasional horse parties, it was in good condition.

Having encouraged me by turning north for a while, the track eventually turned determinedly south and became hard to follow. Reluctantly I retraced my steps, annoyed to have walked a good four miles out of my way. In the other direction the track crossed the river; here it was strong, deep, muddy, and unfordable. Posts on the bank were the only signs that there had once been a bridge.

No other option was available, so I left the tracks and headed north beside the river, climbing high up to a grassy bluff where it cut deeply into the bank. A golden eagle suddenly took off twenty feet in front of me, huge and magnificent. From the bluff I had good views up and down the river and east to a large unnamed lake. When the bluff dropped away to the river I did too, heading for a clump of spruce I thought might harbor a good campsite. It did, but on reaching it I saw a large logjam stretching right across the river. Feeling that this makeshift bridge should not be spurned, I ventured across. It was quite solid, although the water beneath was deeper than my staff, and I crossed easily, then made camp among small lodgepole pines and aspens on a bluff.

I was now just three and a half miles from the highway. For the moment I'd had enough of bushwhacking, trails that led into swamps and vanished, and tracks that enticed me miles in the wrong direction. Next morning, on reaching the shores of the large lake to the east, I found a pack trail leading south to a jeep track, the continuation of the one I'd followed the day before but this time going in the right direction. I took it north to where it crossed clear, placid Klusha Creek, only a few miles from its confluence with the Nordenskiöld River, on a rickety old bridge. The first paintbrush flowers were just emerging, a deep crimson against the green track-side grasses.

Half an hour later I reached the Klondike Highway about a

mile north of Twin Lakes and thirty miles south of Carmacks. It was eight and a half days since I had left Takhini hot springs and I had seen no one during that time. With my skin burned by the sun, my legs scarred with scratches, my hair tangled and matted, and my clothes dirty, I felt painfully conspicuous as I began the trudge up the highway. The steady trickle of big trucks, pickups, and cars seemed incredibly noisy, and the stench of exhaust was overpowering. A few people waved, and I waved back. The road ran through an avenue of tall spruce and aspen. There wasn't much to look at. Empty drink cans clanged underfoot. To pass the time, I collected brands: Coca-Cola, Pepsi-Cola, Mott's Clamato, V8, Sun-Rype Apple Juice, 7-Up, Fanta, Hines, Kokanee, Budweiser. A sign read: Up to $500 Fine for Depositing Litter on the Highway. It was surrounded by cans.

Another, more interesting, sign read Northern Tutchone Trading Post. Open 8–10 Daily. 30 Mi. "I'll be there before closing time tomorrow," I wrote in my journal. Finding a campsite that evening was a problem, mainly because most of the roadside creeks were dry. I finally managed to find a flattish spot in a spruce and aspen grove above a small trickle of a stream out of sight of the road. I could still hear the dull growl of the traffic. Later that evening I climbed the hillside above and worked out from the map and the view that I was camped by Coal Creek and had therefore walked over twenty miles. Carmacks was just eighteen miles away.

A bald eagle floating silently overhead reminded me next morning that the highway was only a slight scar in a vast wilderness. Soon afterward I saw a parked vehicle and two road workers digging. I would have to speak to them. Immediately I considered making a wide loop through the bush to avoid them. I had spoken to no one for nine and a half days and found the idea of doing so intimidating. I walked on, mentally preparing myself for the ordeal of communicating with other people. I doubted I could escape with a brief greeting, walkers being rare on this highway.

They saw me long before I was within hailing distance. As

soon as they could they called me over. "What the hell are you doing?" Once I'd broken my silence, talking seemed ridiculously easy and I couldn't understand why I'd been so worried. The two men showed great interest in my walk and made various helpful suggestions for the route beyond Carmacks. One of them took part in the Yukon Quest each winter, a long-distance wilderness dogsled race held between Whitehorse and Fairbanks, Alaska ("much tougher than the Iditarod"), and he recommended the sled route as a good way to Dawson City. From his outline it sounded the same as my original plan. His most useful advice was to consult Pier at the Forest Service office in Carmacks, who knew the area well. After a welcome refreshing drink of water and lemon from a cold flask, I said farewell and continued along the road.

At 3:00 P.M. I passed a sign reading Entering Carmacks Village. This was a relief to my hot, sore feet. It took forty-five long minutes more to reach the center of the tiny settlement. The Carmacks Hotel had a nice white wooden frontage and cabins for rent at the rear. I booked in for two nights and was soon enjoying a blissful long soak in hot water, my first proper wash for eleven days. I recovered my food bags from behind the bar where George had left them just a few days earlier. And the two stores in town could provide more supplies. The post office was open only from nine to two on Mondays, Wednesdays, and Fridays. Luckily for me I had arrived on a Thursday.

I needed a couple of days' rest, as my feet were battered and sore, with three blisters on my left foot and two on my right. They had all appeared during the road walk. I had, anyway, plenty of time. My food drop at Fort Selkirk was fixed by the *Youcon Kat*'s sailing schedule for twelve days hence. With only eighty miles to walk, most of it probably on good tracks, I could likely have been there in four days.

Thunderstorms and brilliant sunshine marked my first day at Carmacks. I spent it doing essential chores. Laundry first. My clean body cried out for clean clothes. Decently clad, I wandered over to the post office and collected my mail, the first contact with home I'd had for two weeks. It was hard to relate to news of people and places so far away in distance, time, and, crucially, in relation to my frame of mind, which was locked into the wilderness, committed to living in the bush.

Taking the advice I had been given, I visited the Forest Service office and talked to Pier, a weather-beaten man in his mid-thirties. He looked and sounded as though he knew what he was talking about. He had flown all over that area, he told me, and used to travel it regularly on the ground. He suggested I cross the Yukon River at Fort Selkirk, as there were good tracks on the far side that led all the way to the Klondike. The restoration work party at Fort Selkirk would probably take me across, he said. The reason I had originally abandoned this route was the need to cross the Stewart River later. "There are prospectors in the area," said Pier, "so you should be able to find someone to take you over, perhaps the guy working at Barker Creek." He knew of no track on the west bank of the river beyond Fort Selkirk and reckoned the bushwhacking would be desperate, so I adopted his plan and phoned Youcon Tours to ask Red Grossinger to drop all my supplies at Fort Selkirk rather than Stewart Island.

Carmacks is named for George Washington Carmacks, who, with Skookum Jim and Tagish Charlie, discovered gold in the Klondike in 1896 and precipitated the gold rush. Previously he had found coal in the Tantalus Butte area near the Yukon River and his cabin site there became the settlement bearing his name. Unlike many other towns from gold-rush days, Carmacks, although still small, has survived because of the Whitehorse–Dawson highway. Before that it was a stop for riverboats sailing the Yukon. Now canoeists following the river down to Dawson City put in to resupply and stay at the riverbank campground. But there isn't much to Carmacks other than the hotel, restaurant, two stores, and a scattering of houses.

5

Along the
Yukon River

CARMACKS TO FORT SELKIRK

JULY 15–24, 80 MILES

Warm sun, clear water, lazy camps, jumping fish, friendly currents and most of all that much treasured solitude are what I know.

—Gus Karpes, *The Upper Yukon River*

A breakfast of *heuvos rancheros* (eggs in chili sauce) was my last luxury before setting off on the longest section between towns—and restaurants. So far I had walked 260 miles in twenty-six days (of which five had been rest days) passing through Carcross and Whitehorse, and ending in Carmacks. In the next twenty days, three of which would be rest days, I would walk the same distance without crossing a road or passing through a settlement. Although I would pass near Minto, it would be on the other side of the river. This long wilderness sojourn would be possible only by having a food drop at Fort Selkirk.

The first twelve miles out of Carmacks were on a graded gravel road in densely wooded terrain well west of the river. There was little to break up the solid green of the forest, and I walked at a brisk pace. I stopped for the day after only nine miles, however, as I wouldn't see water again for another nine miles. There was no need to hurry: my food supplies wouldn't arrive at Fort Selkirk for another nine days. People were fishing at the first of two lakes I came to, and it showed signs of much use, so I continued down a narrow trail to the second, which lay in a bowl below the road. The shore was narrow and boggy and the banks steep, and I could find nowhere suitable for a camp. Popular or not, it had to be the first lake. By the time I got back, the people had gone and I was alone.

The grassy shore, sadly, had been grossly misused by anglers. The first campsite I found was strewn with litter, the trees and bushes around it trampled, broken, and hacked up. Cans and plastic bags drifted at the water's edge, and long tangles of fishing line were threaded through the reeds. I spent half an hour gathering garbage and burning it in a large fire pit that disfigured the grass. Even so, the site was too depressing and I sought another. As I made my way around the lake, I found several well-used campsites, though none as abused as the first. I eventually stopped at the north end of the lake, lit another fire in yet another fire ring built on the grass, and again burned large amounts of litter and several charred logs.

The lake itself, once I looked beyond the degraded campsites, was beautifully situated. Steep grassy slopes dotted with small groves of trees rose above its eastern shore, and a narrow strip of long grass backed by woods ran around its edge. The placid water, ruffled only occasionally by stray breezes, the white wisps of cloud in the deep blue sky, the protective ring of gentle wooded hills, and the late afternoon heat gave the place a sheltered, peaceful air.

Once I had established camp and set my pans in place over the fire, I settled down to watch the lake come back to life as the effect of my presence slowly receded. Swallows skimmed the surface and bright dragonflies hunted in the reed beds while a small flock of black ducks with orange beaks, either white-winged or surf scoters, swam near the far bank.

I was drifting into peaceful reverie when the evening calm was brutally shattered. A pickup stopped on the road and half a dozen rifle shots rang out, the first one terrifying me, as it was so unexpected and so very loud, its echo bouncing off the hills. Water spurted as bullets bit the lake. The onslaught was over in a few minutes. The unknown assailants slammed the doors and drove off, leaving a trail of feathers on the water and the floating body of a dead duck. More, fainter shots then sounded, probably fired at the waterfowl on a lake I had lunched by earlier.

Peace returned quickly to the scene, but the sudden, wanton killing left me flooded with impotent anger and frustration. A loon flew in and landed in a long spray of water, distracting me from the corpse drifting slowly toward the reeds in front of my camp. A walk around the lake helped ease the tension but had me worrying about bears—though I saw no signs of any—as I found not far from my camp the rotting skull of a dead horse and patches of skin and large hanks of coarse hair.

The stroll also revealed the lake's attraction to anglers—it had been stocked with trout.

Because of the high usage of the lake, I boiled my drinking water; nevertheless, I woke during the night with diarrhea. Pickups passed by several times during the early hours. I left without regret early the next morning. Five miles down the road I turned away from the pickups and the desecration that always seem to accompany easily accessible wilderness to continue the uneventful forest walk on a jeep track.

Eight more miles brought me to Yukon Crossing, so called because the Dawson Road used to cross the Yukon River there, by ferry (hand rowed) in summer and on the ice in winter. The Yukon Crossing route was much shorter than the river. The crossing is 144 miles from Whitehorse by road, 236 by the river. The riverboats stopped here too, but when the Klondike Highway was built, the tiny settlement was abandoned. All that now remain are the massive timbered shells of the old roadhouse and a barn, still roofed but half hidden in dense vegetation. The place is used regularly as a campsite by canoeists paddling from Whitehorse to Dawson. In following the river the rest of the way to Fort Selkirk, I would probably be sharing my camps with other wilderness travelers for the first time since the Chilkoot Trail.

Almost at the same moment I glimpsed the first gray-blue swirl of the river I saw two people pitching a dome tent. They were canoeists from Fairbanks, but I didn't learn much more about them. Our conversation was interrupted by a crack of thunder and a sudden downpour. I hurried on to set up camp. The rain lasted for only half an hour, and a fine fresh evening followed. The site was idyllic, with masses of tall pink fireweed and blue larkspur brightening the greens and yellows of the long grasses. The steady hum of bees and other insects further spoke of the somnolence of high summer.

Two more canoeists arrived and set up their tunnel tent not far from me. I wandered over to say hello and ended up swapping stories for several hours. Louisa Blair and Don Hembroff were from Toronto and doing the classic canoe trip from Whitehorse to Dawson City. For Don this was a short journey; in the 1970s he had spent six years sailing around the world. Like Matti and Erkki on the Chilkoot Trail, they were videotaping their trip. The next morning they slipped off gently in their canoe before I began my own walk along the banks of the Yukon River.

The fourth longest river in North America and the fifth largest in volume of water flow, the Yukon is unique in that its source is just fifteen miles from the Pacific Ocean, in the Coastal Mountains of British Columbia, yet its journey back to that ocean is more than two thousand miles long. Its course defines the shape of the northwest as it meanders across the Yukon Territory and Alaska, curving northwestward to touch the Arctic Circle, then back southwest to salt water at Norton Sound on the Bering Sea. Its length and size made it the key to the exploration of the North American northwest; together with its tributaries the Yukon provides access to 70 percent of the Yukon Territory. The river was crucial to the area's development, until the coming of modern roads and the internal-combustion engine.

The name *Yukon* was first given to the river by the Hudson's Bay Company trader John Bell in 1846 when he reached it from the east via the Porcupine River. It is taken from the native word *yuchoo,* which means "the great river." Bell was not the first European to see the river; Russian trader Andrey Glazunov had traveled part of the lower Yukon in 1835. Alexander Mackenzie had learned of its existence some forty years earlier from natives as he explored the river he gave his name to, across the mountains to the east in the Northwest Territories.

The first white explorers to arrive found the upper Yukon River, the first five hundred miles from the headwaters to Dawson City, controlled by the Chilkat Indians, who were reluctant to let anyone threaten their trading monopoly. But pressure built up for a shorter and more direct route to the rumored goldfields than the river's mouth provided, and in 1880 the first party of miners crossed Chilkoot Pass and drifted downriver on the understanding that they wouldn't do any trading. Three years passed before Lieutenant Frederick Schwatka traveled the river from end to end, making it the last major river in North America to be explored.

During Schwatka's 1883 U.S. Army expedition, topographer Charles A. Homan made the first survey of the river's course, which was later published along with Schwatka's account of the venture. Above its confluence with the Pelly, the river had been known to nonnative visitors before the Schwatka expedition as the Lewes, a name given to it in 1843 by fur trader Robert Campbell after his boss, John Lee Lewes, the chief factor, or chief agent, of the Hudson's Bay Company. Campbell considered the upper Yukon a tributary of the Pelly. As usual Schwatka ignored convention and called the river the Yukon. The name stuck and in 1898 was also attributed to the entire territory, created by the huge influx of people arriving for the gold rush. Amazingly, it was not until 1945 that the river's name was officially changed from Lewes.

The river retained its gold-rush role as the major highway of the Yukon Territory until the building of the roadways in the 1950s, with up to 250 sternwheelers carrying passengers and goods between the many trading posts and small settlements that sprang up on its shores. Now, like the Chilkoot Trail, the river is returning

to wilderness, and the signs of its commercial significance are fading. The last riverboat bore its load of freight and passengers along
the Yukon in 1956. Indeed, as the native peoples who once lived
along it shores have in the main moved to settlements along the
highways, the environs of the river are probably wilder than they
have been for many centuries.

"Yukon" still has a magic ring to it, redolent of the romance
and excitement of the wild northlands, and now that it is a wild
river again, travelers can rediscover the awe of the first explorers: I
was certainly looking forward to my walk along its banks.

The topo map showed a path running along the riverbank from
Yukon Crossing, but the steep-sided rocky bluff dropping straight
into the water on the far side of Crossing Creek made its existence
seem unlikely. I wasn't surprised when I could find no trace of it
and had to bypass the bluff on its landward side. There a wide,
straight track materialized. It stayed well in from the river all the
way to Merrice Creek, where a side trail led to an old cabin and
campsites on the bank, and then on to Williams Creek, where there
used to be a copper mine.

There I hit problems. The wide track disappeared (as Gus
Karpes says in his guide to the upper Yukon River, it "goes from
nowhere to nowhere"), though there were signs of a path following
the waterline. Progress was nearly impossible, however. A dense
tangle of springy willows grew between the river and loose shaley
cliffs that rose just a few feet back from the water's edge. After a
quarter-mile of arduous bushwhacking, I decided I'd rather climb
the steep slopes above than continue thrashing through this jungle.
A five- or six-hundred-foot scrabble during which I didn't look
down led to another desperate bushwhack across thickly wooded
slopes and an equally desperate, loose, slow, sliding, steep descent.
I arrived at the river after three hours, totally exhausted and barely a
mile beyond Williams Creek.

But here the cut line reappeared. I followed it to the trickle of
almost-dry Hoo-Che-Koo Creek and camped right on the track, the

forest around being thick with brush. It wasn't the most scenic site but, as I wrote in my journal, "I have a fire, it's shady, and it's flat, and at 9:30 P.M., after 14 miles, who could want more?" It had been a long, hard day. Ironically, even though this felt like a remote wilderness spot, I could hear the constant rumble of traffic. Less than two miles away, hidden in the trees across the river, lay the Klondike Highway.

A woodpecker carefully prospected the trunk of a spruce tree near my camp, and squirrels chattered as I ate my breakfast. It's too hot for walking, I thought, feeling even more lazy than I usually did first thing in the morning. "The after-effects of yesterday, I suppose," my journal entry says, though in retrospect my lethargy was also probably heat induced. This was the hottest day so far, and it was still eighty degrees Fahrenheit at 9:30 that evening. I didn't leave until noon but still felt tired all day. Clumsy, constantly tripping over roots, I found concentrating on the details of walking difficult. Recognizing that some days just don't work out right, even in the wilderness, I made camp after just nine miles.

The map showed no water for many miles, so I had drunk two pints of coffee before setting off and carried a quart of water. I spent most of the day on the overgrown cut track, which cut through the forest well away from the river. There was much bear sign, both dung and fresh diggings where plants had been uprooted, and I kept a careful lookout.

The track terminated abruptly at the edge of a dry, overgrown streambed. It may have continued upstream, but my main concern was to find water, not the route, so I headed downstream toward the Yukon and a fine, dry camp on a flat bluff some thirty feet above the river that gave a good view upstream. The site had been used before, though not recently. A couple of fire rings and ax-cut timber lay among the masses of beaver-felled aspens.

I lit a fire and spent the evening drinking gallons of liquid, mainly coffee. I had bought instant hot chocolate in Carmacks, which I was now regretting; I didn't find the thick, sweet drink refreshing. Lemonade powder would have been a welcome alternative.

From the vast gray river came constantly shifting sounds, as if the Yukon were a huge living creature. Swirls and pools swept past, coming and going in momentary existence. I watched the moving surface as I would the flames of a fire, hypnotized by the infinitely variable patterns. A beaver swam downstream, perfectly at home in the powerful currents. Sandpipers bobbed and called at the water's edge, and martins skimmed the surface.

I drifted off to sleep with the sleeping bag draped over me, to wake at 5:30 A.M. feeling slightly chilly in the delightfully cool dawn light. The temperature was fifty degrees. Ideal for walking, I thought, suddenly realizing that I usually walked in the heat of the day, between noon and eight in the evening. "I must be mad," I wrote at the time, though I didn't change my habits. The slow, yellow sunrise, simultaneously spectacular and subtle, distracted me, and I shot nearly a roll of film as the world gained definition and the soft blurs of the night became the hard edges of daylight.

I still managed to leave at the early hour, for me, of 8:00 A.M. Despite the sun I was clad in long pants and windproof jacket in expectation of a day of bushwhacking. Within a few hours I was soaked in sweat. I lunched across the river from the tiny village of Minto, where the Klondike Highway leaves the river and heads north. I was not to see or hear traffic again until I reached Dawson.

The summer heat continued to build. By two it was eighty-three degrees in the shade. "The sky is hazy with heat and so am I," I wrote in my journal just before turning inland to cut behind a "rock" that rose three hundred feet straight out of the river. I admired the brightly colored shining pebbles of Big Creek as I forded its knee-deep, fast-flowing clear waters. The bridge had collapsed long ago. The far bank was so dense with bushes that during the half-mile walk downstream to the Yukon I forded Big Creek fifteen times. Wading was easier than bushwhacking.

A shingle bank at the head of the creek made a good campsite with excellent views across the Yukon, marred only by the swarms of mosquitoes bred, no doubt, in the willow-thicketed swamps on either side. Mosquito coils and the smoke from my driftwood fire kept them at bay. My last ford of the creek had been crotch deep, so I stripped and hung out pants, underpants, and socks to dry. Despite the high clouds, the heat was still intense, eighty degrees at 8:30 P.M.—no need for clothes. Four canoes passed down the Yukon during the evening, but none stopped to camp. Gus Karpes tells of a legend that gold stolen from the Klondike goldfields is buried somewhere around here. I was too hot to consider searching for it.

An eagle landing on a snag at the mouth of the creek did stir me to creep toward it, tripod and camera in hand, to take several pictures as the magnificent bird perched motionless staring out across the river. I thought it was a golden eagle, but many months later a knowledgeable member of the audience at a showing of my slides pronounced it an immature bald eagle.

In the morning the sky was hazy, cloudless, and still. Despite the heat I relit the fire, both to save fuel and to keep the mosquitoes away. A vast amount of driftwood and the shingle bank scoured regularly by the creek freed me from worrying about the impact. The noise of an engine had me looking up to see a motorboat flash past, soon followed by another.

With no sign of a path, I plunged into the willow swamps and stagnant backwaters behind my camp, not a pleasant start to the day. Once I escaped them I found the flat shady forest rich in vegetation and mostly free of the deadfall that impedes progress. The walking was almost hypnotic in the still silence of the trees. The only sounds were the infrequent chatter of a squirrel and the faint hum of insects in the occasional sunny clearing. I thought about loneliness, something others seem to feel should be a problem on a long solo walk. I have never found this to be so. In my journal I wrote, "How can you be lonely here? This is the heart of life. A place to be content and at peace while the work of nature, so superior to our efforts, goes on all around."

The power and splendor of the forest almost overwhelmed me. The pale green leaves, orange berries, yellow and red lichen and moss, dusky white aspens, deep russet of split fallen spruce, and all the bright colors of the understory, combined to make a beauty the reason for whose existence I could not grasp. It was enough to share in the magic.

Late in the day a pile of old cut logs lying in the forest led me to a well-blazed, recently maintained trail. Although the path led away from the river and took a tortuous line, I moved more quickly than when I was bushwhacking, and I stayed with it. Eventually the trail passed some grassy knolls, then descended steeply to a small creek, the first running water I had seen for several hours. As I had no idea how far away the next water was, it seemed an obvious place to stop for the night.

From the top of a nearby knoll I could see the Yukon River about half a mile away, but I couldn't work out exactly where I was. I hoped I might be at Wolverine Creek, but I suspected I was actually at a small unnamed creek three miles before Wolverine. It didn't really matter. Whichever it was, I would easily reach Fort Selkirk the next day, three days before my food would arrive.

At two the next afternoon I still didn't know which creek I had camped at, though by then I was many miles away. The trail had returned to the banks of the Yukon, which it then followed past an old decaying hunters' camp with a small hut perched high on a platform of poles. This was a "meat safe" where game was stored out of reach of bears and other animals.

Three boats with bright sails drifted into view. Two of them were catamarans made from canoes with platforms connecting them, the other was a small kayak. The occupants waved. I waved back, then followed the trail to a creek that I guessed was the Wolverine. I crossed it easily on a massive logjam; I could hear but not see gurgling water. As on the day before, I was walking in a dreamlike state, made sleepy by the heat and thinking of nothing.

Beyond the creek the trail started to fade and wander erratically. I lost it a few times as it led to the Yukon, then up onto a bluff, and then back inland. Finally I lost it completely and bushwhacked for an hour before reaching a wide, well-used track that led straight to the ghost town of Fort Selkirk. Wanting to shed my load before looking around, I walked on past the strangely deserted buildings of the old settlement to the campground that lay on the far side.

The site was large and dusty, the bare ground sparsely dotted with clumps of small pines, picnic tables, fire pits, and large piles of cut wood. A cabin stood at one corner. Two large parties of teenage boys with a few adult male leaders were already in noisy residence, and there were clusters of tents at each end of the site. I set up my camp in the middle of a bare patch, feeling exposed. During the evening I spoke to people from each group and found they were from Palmer and Sitka, Alaska. The people from Palmer were the canoe-catamaran group I had seen earlier. Their leader came over for a chat and told me he had been taking groups down the Yukon for many years and had built the catamarans so they could cook on board and erect a tarp when it rained. They usually only landed to sleep, he said. His party of nine had started out on the Teslin River, a tributary of the Yukon upstream from Whitehorse, and were finishing at Dawson. Both parties were moving on the next day, and I determined to bag one of their tree-shaded sites as soon as they left.

As I was cooking supper a small, elderly native man with a lined face topped by a dark-blue peaked cap introduced himself as Danny Roberts, the Yukon Parks Service caretaker of Fort Selkirk, a historic site. I signed the large visitors book he had tucked under his arm. The blood-red sun and the hazy air were due, Danny told me, to smoke from a big forest fire burning two hundred miles to the west at Tok, in Alaska. Fires were apparently also blazing at Mayo to the northeast and on the Dempster Highway far away to the north. At 10:45 P.M., just as I finished photographing the magnificent deep-red sunset, two German canoeists arrived and pitched a small silver tent close to mine. As I was to learn, virtually everyone traveling the river downstream from Whitehorse stops at Fort Selkirk.

A deep, sonorous bird call woke me at 2:00 A.M. I peered out of the tent to see the silhouette of an owl perched in the dead lodge-pole pine opposite my tent. Voices and the clank of pots woke me again at seven as one of the canoe parties packed up. It was cooler in the open than in the forest, the overnight low was forty degrees Fahrenheit. Though the sky was clear, the smoke haze was still heavy and a faint smell of smoke was just detectable in the air. I ambled down to the river to watch the two large parties drift off into the insubstantial horizon. The German canoeists, two young men wearing serious-looking olive-green trousers sporting bulging thigh pockets with long knives strapped to their belts, told me of their travels as they prepared to depart. Their six-week trip had begun with the Chilkoot Trail, after which they hitchhiked to Whitehorse and rented a canoe. The Yukon, they told me as they pushed off into the river, was well known in Germany.

Once they had gone all was quiet for a few hours. A canoe party put in for lunch and offered me a cold can of Rainier beer, a most welcome gift. They were from Vancouver and hoped to reach Dawson in a week. This was only their second day out though; they had started at Minto, only a short distance upstream. Two more canoeists arrived soon afterward, seeking clean water. "There's only the river," I told them.

The visitors gone, I moved my camp to the shelter of shrubby trees where I would at least have early-morning and late-evening shade. I then carefully laid out all my gear, set up a camera and tri-pod, and, using the self-timer, photographed myself standing next to it all. Whenever I look at the picture I realize how much I was carrying—and by that time there was little food among the gear— and wonder how I managed it.

Fort Selkirk is important historically because it was the first nonnative settlement on the upper Yukon River. Robert Campbell of the Hudson's Bay Company founded the fort in 1848 to control the fur trade. He named it after the fifth earl of Selkirk, a town in southern Scotland. Campbell's original post was at the mouth of the Pelly River, just upstream from Fort Selkirk and on the far bank. That site was prone to flooding, and four years later Campbell moved the post to the present spot. That summer, however, the Chilkats, fearing the threat to their trading monopoly, attacked and looted the fort, being careful not to hurt any of the inhabitants. Without sufficient food to survive the winter, Campbell abandoned the post and made his mammoth snowshoe trek to Quebec. The attack, the only one of its kind to occur in the Yukon, was a Chilkat success, as the Hudson's Bay Company refused Campbell's request to reestablish the fort; they didn't return to the area for more than fifty years.

In 1889, Irish pioneer Arthur Harper, one of the first prospectors in the Yukon Territory, set up a trading post on the site, then known as Campbell's Fort. Harper had previously explored the White River and other rivers in the area—including several where gold was later found, but without success.

Harper's trading post developed into a small town during the gold rush and in 1898 Fort Selkirk, as it was again called, became the headquarters of the Yukon Field Force, part of the Canadian army. The site was considered as a possible capital of the Yukon, but the recall of the soldiers just a year later and the decline in population with the end of the gold rush prevented Fort Selkirk from achieving that distinction.

River traffic kept the community alive until the 1950s, when the new highway from Whitehorse to Dawson made river travel obsolete. The inhabitants abandoned Fort Selkirk, moving to the new settlement of Pelly Crossing, where the highway crosses the Pelly River.

Fort Selkirk began to decay and fade back into the forest, but in the 1980s work crews from the Selkirk Indian band, now based at Pelly Crossing, restored the town. This work is still continuing, and the site is a cross between a museum and a ghost town, looking, I suppose, at least a little as it must have just forty or so years ago, though to my European eyes it looks far older.

I strolled down the wide, dusty main street past the weather-faded wooden houses and stores, their cool, sparsely decorated interiors providing an inkling of what life must have been like. In the harsh but hazy smoke-dimmed light, the silent street had an air of unreality, of being out of time, and I half expected to see gold-rush pioneers come staggering out of the stores, burdened with picks and shovels.

Thunder rumbled sullenly somewhere to the north as I ambled back to the campground, sticky with sweat. A hot upstream breeze only added to the discomfort. The temperature in the sun was 120 degrees Fahrenheit. I had an afternoon snack of cream of broccoli soup. I was running out of some supplies, but I had lots of soup. I always had lots of soup.

To escape the full glare of the sun I took the soup and a book to the small shelter cabin and sat on a bench shaded by the porch. Across the river a line of basalt cliffs rose out of the water, while downstream I could see the massive bulk of 200-foot Victoria Rock, the only real landmark in the area.

Danny Roberts came and told me that he was expecting the work crew back at any time. They worked for ten days, then had four days off, and this was the last day of their leave. He also confirmed that the trail on this bank of the river was overgrown and hard to follow. The last river trip he had made to Dawson had been in 1961, and he had once guided a party overland from Carmacks. Looking through his visitors book, which went back to 1985, I saw that Matti and Erkki had been through three weeks before me. Most of the entries were by people from Canada and the United States, but surprisingly large numbers of Germans and Swiss and a few Norwegians had also come through. Britain seemed to produce about one visitor a year. There were no other hikers, but there was one entry from a woman who had come overland with a dogsled in winter. Fifty-two people, including me, had stopped here in the last four days.

At 10:00 P.M. my peaceful, half-awake, drifting day came to an abrupt end as the work crew came down the Pelly, then across the Yukon in flat-bottomed riverboats powered by outboard motors. The first of five boats arrived with news of a moose sighting on an island just upstream. Several of the crew set off immediately with Danny to see if they could shoot it. While they were away, one of the other crew members recognized me from the piece in the *Yukon News,* now more than a month old. He offered me sun- and smoke-dried moose meat, which he said was good for the trail. It required prolonged chewing but was quite tasty. A second, more crowded boat arrived containing children and their mothers, cooks for the work crew. They opened the kitchen at once and made coffee. The kitchen, along with their cabins and workshops, was hidden in the trees on the edge of the campground.

I was drinking coffee and answering questions about how I survived in the bush and why I didn't carry a rifle, something that amazed them, when a shot rang out. Everyone paused. The expressions on all the faces asked the same question. Had they killed the moose? The breeze became cooler as the sun, again blood red in the smoky air, slowly sank into the river, sending shafts of crimson along the water.

Two of the work crew suggested I cross the Yukon to continue my journey, going up the Pelly a few miles to Pelly Farm, where I could pick up the old Dawson Trail. Danny would probably take me there, they said. They confirmed that walking farther on this side of the river would be difficult. I asked about crossing the Stewart River, my only concern about the Dawson Trail route. One of them thought that members of a Christian community on the far side of Maisy May Creek would ferry me across. Between this group and the prospector at Barker Creek that Pier had mentioned in Carmacks, I had two possibilities for crossing the Stewart.

A few more shots rang out, then the would-be hunters returned. They hadn't even seen the moose, but one of them had fired his rifle anyway. It quickly became apparent that he was drunk and probably couldn't have shot a moose if it had walked into him.

Young, with long black hair, a black T-shirt advertising Harley-Davidson motorcycles, and black jeans, he looked as though he would be more at home in a city than in the wilderness. Producing a bottle of vodka, he proceeded to get increasingly more drunk and garrulous. Insisting I visit his cabin, he gave me two large candles that I accepted because I didn't know how to refuse them tactfully. Then, with me in tow, he raided the kitchens for fruit juice. There he pressed a large box of kitchen matches on me, first opening the upside-down box to see if it were full. It was.

As soon as I could, I crept away unnoticed, but my drunken new-found friend soon followed me. "Let's have a fire," he cried, on seeing the ashes of the one I had lit earlier. He staggered off, to return in a few minutes with an empty cardboard beer crate he dumped in the fire pit and lit. Once this was ablaze he picked up all the wood I had so neatly stacked for the next day and dumped the lot on top. The flames leaped several feet in the air, and we had to stand well back to avoid being burned. A piece of woods lore I had heard years before came into my mind. The gist of it was that a white man builds a big fire and stands away from it but an Indian has a small fire and crouches over it, the latter being the better way. In this case it was the Indian who wanted the bonfire. Finally at half past midnight I managed to sneak off to bed. It had been an entertaining evening.

Jays scampering on the picnic table, their claws clacking on the painted surface, woke me early. I drifted back to sleep to be woken again by the bell for the work crew. With no need to get up, I dozed until midmorning, when hunger forced me up to breakfast on the last of the granola. One of the workers I hadn't met the previous night stopped by to talk. "Hi, I'm J. Roger Alfred," he said, holding out his hand. I guessed him to be in his mid-thirties. He had a light but muscular build, hooded, serious eyes, and a faint smile. His blue jeans, check shirt, and large straw cowboy hat reminded me of the outfitters I'd met on my walk through the Canadian Rockies two years earlier. I wasn't surprised when he told me he ran pack tours under the name Northern Tutchone Outfitters, which takes people into the wilderness to photograph game or to hike from a base camp. He too had read the piece in the *Yukon News* and was interested in the walk and the gear I was using.

Where the day before had mostly been one of silence and solitude, on this day Fort Selkirk was busy, with a generator humming in the background, minitractors and other work vehicles chugging about, and a large fire for burning cleared brush blazing by the river. I noticed my friend from the night before. He glanced sheepishly at me. I guessed he was nursing a hangover and probably trying to remember what he had done. Two Germans were the first canoeists of the day to call in. The work crew, I noticed, referred to visitors as tourists, which I suppose we all were, though I tend to think of tourism as a more passive activity than canoeing or walking. Danny appeared at the Germans' side, asking them to sign his book. Now I knew why he carried it around all the time.

After the Germans departed, Danny came over to talk. The fire at Tok was still out of control, and another threatened the native village of Old Crow in the northern Yukon. As there is no road access there, the inhabitants had been evacuated by air. A powerboat with four people on board roared upstream. "They're from Ballarat Creek where there's a successful gold mine," said Danny. Three more Germans on an outboard-motor-powered rubber raft arrived, and Danny went off to collect their signatures.

Stuffing dried moose meat into my pockets, I set off in the afternoon along the good trail to Victoria Rock, an impressive cliff more than two hundred feet high and six hundred or so feet long running inland from the river. It had many sheer faces and large buttresses, plus corners, arêtes, and gullies. If it were in a more accessible spot it would be covered with rock climbers. There was no trace of a trail beyond the rock, so I returned to Fort Selkirk confident that crossing the river there would be the right decision. It meant breaking the walk briefly, but bushwhacking all the way to Dawson didn't appeal, if indeed it was even possible, and I'd miss the Klondike goldfields. As I couldn't walk on water, a boat was the only way across the river.

Several people were at the campground when I got back, including a couple on a day trip from Minto, twenty-four miles upstream. Felix, who ran the boat trips, recommended the route from Pelly Farm as the best overland one to Dawson and told me he had heard the *Youcon Kat* was due in Minto soon for refueling. As he and his clients set off back upriver one of them called out, only half jokingly it seemed, "Do you have a TV or a VCR? I couldn't hike without them." I shook my head as much in disbelief as denial. Only as they disappeared from view did it occur to me I should have gone with them to Minto both to see the river from a different perspective and to buy supplies. I cursed myself on and off for the rest of the day for missing this chance, especially as I hadn't much to do. The temperature, at one hundred, was too hot for anything active anyway.

Now that I had decided on a route to Dawson, I spread out my maps, weighing down the corners with stones to stop them flapping in the breeze, and studied them more closely. The track was clearly marked and involved little ascent. The distance from Pelly Farm to Dawson looked to be about 150 miles, though I couldn't be certain. A short section of the track was not on any of the maps. Furthermore, I had only 1:250,000 maps for the next section, having exchanged the 1:50,000 ones back in Whitehorse for maps covering the route along the river. But now I was back on the route I had worked out in Britain. Given my rate of progress so far, about ten days' walking would be enough to reach Dawson on August 3, three days ahead of schedule. Coming on the *Youcon Kat* I had fifteen days' worth of food. I decided to ask Red if he would take the surplus down to Dawson. Five days' food meant ten pounds of unnecessary weight, and my pack was too heavy anyway. I hoped I had put several books in the supply box, as I had run out. Luckily I was able to swap my last one, John Le Carré's *Russia House,* for two books from the work crew, one a cheap thriller I ended up not reading, and the other, to my great surprise, a battered copy of *Lady Chatterley's Lover.*

A family of two adults and two children arrived in a motorboat and proceeded to make camp. I watched in amazement as they set up a large frame tent, then produced a table and tablecloth, chairs, a Calor gas burner, and much more. This was definitely the luxury approach to camping. The man came over for a chat, as did nearly everyone who arrived. He was unlike all the other people I had met in the Yukon; although superficially friendly, he had an irritating and superior manner, and he made it clear he didn't believe I had really hiked there. He was the first person I met whom I immediately disliked.

As I watched the luxury campers trying to light a fire, Roger came over again with fresh food—a slab of fruit cake, a slice of apple pie, a scone, and an apple—for which I was most grateful. Dried soup several times a day was beginning to pall. I ate the cake and scone at once but kept the other food for breakfast. Roger stayed to talk. Earlier in the evening he had been out on the river looking for moose. Although he hadn't found any, he had seen two grizzlies on the large island that lay just upstream from Fort Selkirk. "Keep upwind of them and you'll be safe," was his advice on bears in general.

He went on to tell me about the tours he ran. They included fishing trips, photo hunts of big game, and programs to teach bushcraft and natural medicine, combined with both hiking and horse travel. One of his aims was to give the native people's perspective on wilderness living. "We live here year-round," he pointed out, "but most white outfitters don't and haven't the same knowledge or understanding of the region."

For six years Roger was a hunting guide, but he gave up the work because of the compromises he had to make. Native people, he said, use all of the animals they take, wasting nothing, unlike white trophy hunters. He made the same point about trapping, which wasn't understood in Europe he said; when done by natives it wasn't inhumane or wasteful. I listened without comment. While against trapping in principle, I could see his point about the lifestyles of native peoples and their traditional closeness to nature, which gave them a different attitude toward wildlife than that of other hunters and trappers. Our talk created a dilemma for me I still haven't resolved. It was clear that Roger and I shared a sense of the value of wilderness, but while I, coming from a culture where such a view had been long suppressed, was learning this anew, he was fighting to retain the close link with nature that had been the norm for his people for centuries. Roger's words showed a sense of pride in his heritage and a great concern for the future of the native peoples of Canada.

Taking a folding short-bladed knife from a sheath on his belt, Roger sliced off a piece of bark from a nearby spruce tree and peeled off the white inside. This, he said, could be boiled to make an infusion that was good for many internal disorders, from cancer to colds. You could also put the sticky pitch of the spruce on a septic cut or sore as a cure or even chew it if an internal antiseptic was needed.

Roger's eyes lit up as he talked of his winter activities, when he ran a dog team and set out on the dogsled racing circuit. A professional musher, as the racers are called, Roger said he preferred the short sprint races, for which there was a North American championship, to the longer, better-known Iditarod and Yukon Quest. He described the latter as easy and said he would leave them until he was older, in his fifties maybe.

Racing requires careful attention to detail, and mushers need to know when to feed their dogs and what wax to use on their sled runners, and to be able to predict the weather. During the previous year he had, for the first time, entered an event in Alaska that consisted of a series of races run over a number of days. He had been pleased to come in fifth out of twenty-seven. Roger made it clear that he was ambitious, but said that expectations of natives were high in these races and the pressure was great. He also led dogsled tours in the winter, with the sled carrying food and gear and his clients skiing or snowshoeing.

When we continued our conversation the next day, we took up the subject of mining, since I was headed for the Klondike. Roger's was not a romantic view. He was concerned that miners were polluting the rivers. His voice was hard with anger when he told me they use cyanide in the gold extraction process. He was also concerned about a proposed oil pipeline from Inuvik in the Northwest Territories coming through the Yukon; Louisa Blair at Yukon Crossing, had expressed this same fear. A pipeline, he said, would disrupt the migration of the great caribou herds of the north. This subject led us on to reindeer and the effects of the Chernobyl nuclear disaster on the reindeer-herding Sami, the native people of northern Scandinavia.

The man from the luxury camp came by to ask the whereabouts of sandbars farther downriver; he had already run aground once. Roger went quiet at his approach, his face almost expressionless, his dislike tangible. He answered the man's questions tonelessly, with the minimum number of words. The articulate, passionate, concerned person I had been talking with for two days had vanished. In his place was a sullen, unhelpful, and apparently dullwitted man. Once the visitor left, Roger exploded with a blast of scathing comments. He mentioned no names, but I guessed he knew who the man was and something of what he did. "That," he spat out, "was a rich man from Whitehorse, playing at being in the wilderness." He and his kind threatened the land and the traditions of the native people and had no understanding of them.

I spent most of the day scanning the river for the *Youcon Kat,* though I knew it probably wouldn't arrive before late afternoon. A large canoe party rolled in at three, the five canoes bearing ten people. David, the leader, told me it was a six-day tour organized by Rainbow Tours/Access Yukon, the organization that had encouraged me many months earlier by their reply to my request for advice regarding my route. "We have more than enough food," he said, when I told him of my walk. "I'm sure you'd like something fresh." With that he loaded me down with cookies, bread, salami, celery, cucumber, and lemonade powder. As I'd already had a large lunch of mushroom soup, flan, sausage, and chips courtesy of the work crew kitchen staff, I suddenly found myself with an abundance of food—not that I considered for a second rejecting any of it; the change was a relief. Later Danny came over and told me that a young grizzly had wandered into Fort Selkirk that morning but had run off when Danny went outside to see what his dog was barking at.

While I watched and waited, a couple of canoes stopped briefly, one of them bound for the Bering Sea. Finally at five o'clock I caught sight of the small, squat *Youcon Kat,* barely visible on the pale-gray water. Soon Red was swinging his boat into the bank and calling out a greeting. Three passengers leaped ashore to stretch their legs. I drank a beer with Red, who said they had seen Dall sheep and a black bear on the trip and that there were twenty or thirty canoes not far behind him, all heading for Dawson. He gave me a weather forecast too. The hot spell was meant to continue a few more days at least. But the wind had already shifted from southeast to southwest, and high cirrus clouds streaking the sky heralded, I suspected, a more imminent change.

Sorting out my two bags of supplies, I found I had easily enough food for fifteen days but no coffee or sugar. More good fortune—Red's passengers were not keen on coffee or sugar, so he passed on his excess to me. He also agreed to take my surplus supplies and maps to Dawson.

Roger came over for a last conversation while I was repacking my supplies and offered a boat ride over to Pelly Farm the next morning. We talked again about hunting. Roger had once guided a party hunting with bows and arrows. Never again, he said. Many animals were only wounded at first. He remembered a grizzly bear that had run a long way before dropping dead and a maimed bighorn sheep whose throat he had to cut. The key to finding game, whether to shoot, photograph, or simply watch, was to know where the animals habitually gathered. He said, for example, that white-tailed deer often come down to the river on the far shore in the evening. "Keep scanning that bank and you might see one." Later in the evening a white-tailed deer did indeed slip out of the trees and down to the water's edge. If I hadn't been watching for it, I almost certainly wouldn't have seen it. Roger had led big game hunts around the Blackstone and Ogilvie rivers north of Dawson, an area that I would be traversing, so I asked him about river crossings. The Blackstone is really only a creek, he replied, and the Ogilvie should be fordable with care in places.

My last night at Fort Selkirk was the warmest so far; the thermometer went no lower than a sticky, humid sixty degrees. My weather forecast was fulfilled by a light drizzle, the first rain for some time. I woke to find a few new tents on the site, one of them a bright yellow geodesic dome with "Please do not wake up. I am from Japan. I am traveling by bike around Australia" written on it in large letters.

Courtesy of Red I had two fresh eggs for breakfast. I waved him and his passengers farewell as the *Youcon Kat* chugged off downstream, then loaded my heavy pack into Roger's flat-bottomed riverboat for the six-mile trip up the Pelly River. The air was still hazy and the light flat and dull, but the voyage gave good views of the basalt cliffs, lining the banks to the west, before we landed at Pelly Farm. I was glad to continue my walk after the three-day rest. First, though, I had a farm to visit.

FORT SELKIRK TO DAWSON CITY

JULY 25–AUGUST 6, 170 MILES

In the Klondike Valley gold lay more
thickly than on any other creek, river,
pup, or sand-bar in the whole of the
Yukon watershed.

—Pierre Berton, *Klondike:*
The Last Great Gold Rush

6

Into the
Klondike

We were many miles from the nearest road or village, with mile after mile of dense forest stretching away on either side, but as I stepped out of Roger's boat I saw crop-filled fields and a huddle of weather-darkened wood buildings. This was Pelly Farm, a pioneer venture first established in 1901 but, unlike most such settlements, still thriving.

Roger needed to refuel, so I helped him lug his empty jerricans up the bank to the oil barrels. Then we walked out of the bright sunshine and into the main farm building, which was somber and gloomy but pleasantly cool. Several people lingered inside the small, cluttered room, including Hugh, the farmer himself, who was a tall, thin man with a deeply lined face. They had heard I was at Fort Selkirk and were not too surprised to see me. Introductions over and a cup of coffee in hand, I told the story of the walk so far and immediately received advice about my route. The trail to Dawson was a good one, I was told, and I should easily be there in ten days. The first day would have to be a long one, though, as after the first four miles I would find no water for another fifteen. Three

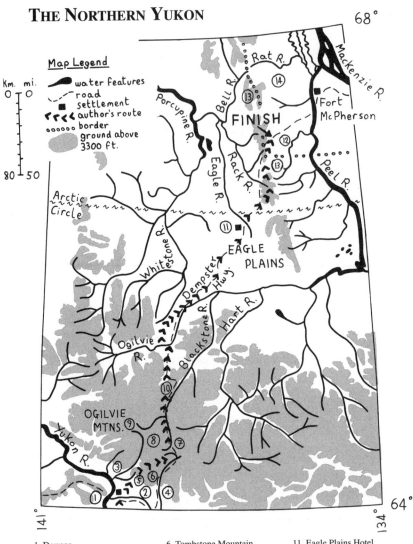

1. Dawson
2. Klondike River
3. Chandindu River
4. North Klondike River
5. Little Twelve Mile River

6. Tombstone Mountain
7. North Fork Pass
8. Cloudy Range
9. Seela Pass
10. Distincta Peak

11. Eagle Plains Hotel
12. Vittrekwa River
13. Richardson Mountains
14. Northwest Territories

days should see me to the Stewart River, where there were prospectors on Scroggie Creek who would probably ferry me across.

The talk then turned to the forest fires that were still burning at

Tok and elsewhere. The air outside was hazy and smelled of smoke. Some of the fires were much nearer than Alaska, I gathered, and I sensed an undercurrent of concern in the apparently casual discussion. With thick forest all around, Pelly Farm could easily be destroyed in a big fire. The talk worried me slightly, too. My route lay toward the fires and was mostly in forest all the way to Dawson. I had once walked into a large fire in the Rocky Mountains in Montana and knew just how hard it was to work out which direction the flames were moving and where to go to be safe from the blaze. On that occasion I had walked for hours on a dusty forest road, trying to get around the fire, until I was found by a fire-fighting crew who drove me out. As we sped through the burning forest, black with charred trees and red with exploding blazing branches, I realized I would have had no chance of surviving if caught in that inferno on foot.

Before I left, Hugh offered to show me around his farm. He had been there thirty-two years and was proud of it, quite rightly in my opinion. I've always thought farming was a hard way to earn a living. To farm successfully out there in the wilderness seemed an amazing achievement. The nearest settlements are at Pelly Crossing, twenty-five miles up the Pelly River, and Minto, twenty-five miles up the Yukon.

Pelly Farm is a mixed enterprise, with a herd of beef cattle, plenty of chickens, a large vegetable plot, and fields for silage, which are also used for wintering outfitters' horses. Salmon are netted from the Pelly; a dozen ten-pounders had been caught the night before and were being gutted on the riverbank preparatory to drying and smoking. As we inspected the neat fields, Hugh told me of his problems with the permafrost that lay a few feet below the surface, which allowed for little running water. When new fields had needed irrigating, Hugh brought in a dowser who successfully located a narrow strip of land under which water was running, even though the ground was frozen solid all around.

As we toured the tidy, carefully hoed and weeded rows of

vegetables—an incongruous sight in this wilderness setting—Hugh gave me fresh carrots and sweet-tasting peas with edible pods, not foods I expected to be offered out here. He also told me about the weather. He had kept detailed records since he had first arrived, and this summer was drier and much hotter than average.

I left the farm and recommenced the walk by midmorning, heading into the rolling wooded hills on a wide dirt track. Within minutes the neat ordered fields vanished and the untamed forest took over. For twenty-two miles of easy if a little uninspiring walking the dense screen of trees rarely parted. The sky was gray with cloud and smoke all day, and it was much cooler. After the temperatures I had become used to, sixty degrees felt chilly.

Toward the end of the day I entered the Black Creek valley. As the track lay in dry forest I bushwhacked down to the slow, turgid backwaters that made up the creek to get water. The banks were a mass of tangled willows, tall grass tussocks, and marshes, and there was nowhere to camp. I filled my two-gallon water bag, protecting it under my pack lid from the spiny vegetation, and retreated to the track.

A short reconnaissance ahead revealed quite a few bear droppings but no sign of even a half-decent campsite, so I stopped at the side of the track, setting up the tent several dozen yards into the forest on roughly level ground. Damp and chilly and in need of a little warmth, I lit a fire in the middle of the track, the only safe, bare area. It had been a long day and I was tired; the pack was heavy with ten days' supplies. After a couple of mugs of coffee and a Leonardo da Fettucini, one of my favorite AlpineAire meals despite the name, I was somewhat restored and began to enjoy the quiet of the forest.

Because I had changed this section of the route several times, I ended up with only 1:250,000 maps for the stretch between Black Creek and Dawson. In fact, for the next day or so I wouldn't have a map at all. Only the many reassurances I had received about the good quality of the track enabled me to proceed without too many qualms. I estimated that until I reached the edge of the next map, my progress would be three and a half miles an hour, a speed I usually maintain on a good path without too much ascent.

A sprinkle of rain fell just as I was dropping off to sleep, a precursor of the heavy rain that woke me at six. The temperature was fifty degrees, and the air was chilly and damp. My previous night's kitchen site was soaked, so I moved everything to a dry patch under a big spruce tree and sat looking out at the somber forest, dark green and dripping. Above, the sky was a forbidding solid gray. My mood matched the weather and motivating myself to pack up was difficult. I finally left at noon in continuing steady rain. The track climbed slowly up the side of the valley, revealing long mist-shrouded green ridges and lumpy, rounded hills. Less than fifteen minutes from my site I passed a stream and a flat cleared area ideal for a camp beside the remains of a cabin. Fresh moose tracks abounded in the mud.

Upon reaching Jane Creek I had left the drainage of the Pelly River for that of the Stewart, though the latter was still a long way off. A long climb took me to the divide between Jane and Walhalla creeks. I intended following Walhalla to Scroggie Creek and then Scroggie to the Stewart River. Beyond the divide I stopped by the first side creek I reached, as there was a cleared space by the trail for a fire and a patch of flat gravel for the tent. Campsites being rare in the wet, dense forest, I knew better than to pass one by.

The site was pleasant, with a bit of a view of forested hills in the distance, but plagued with blackflies—nasty little monsters that gave painful bites and weren't repelled by mosquito coils. The smoke from my fire proved more effective, and I sat close to it. For the first time I had painful sores on each heel, probably caused by walking in wet boots and socks all day. I patched them carefully with Second Skin, a moist slimy substance that is difficult to handle but is the most effective cure I've found for sores and blisters.

Perhaps the most enjoyable parts of a wilderness trip where the walking is easy and the scenery unspectacular are the campsites. I love creating a tiny outdoor haven that for a brief while is home. By now a rough routine had evolved. Central to it was the pack, leaned against a tree or bank or propped up with my staff; this was my backrest. If the ground was damp I laid out the pack cover or my rain jacket in front of the pack as a seat. On my right-hand side I would array my kitchen, which consisted of one red and one gray nylon food sack, a quart-size stainless steel pan, a pint-size stainless steel mug, two spoons, Swiss Army knife, pot scrubber, water containers, matches and lighter, and a rubbish bag. Then I would set up the stove and withdraw from the food bags those items I would be using that evening—coffee, sugar, dried milk, lemonade powder, dried soup, spices, freeze-dried entree. If I had a fire I built it a few feet in front of my seat and placed the folding grill over it.

On my left went my office-cum-study items—maps, paperback books, zip-closed nylon case holding papers, pens, notebook—my camera gear, a smoking mosquito coil if required, thermometer, and if necessary, first-aid kit and repair kit. Other items remained in the pack.

The only variation to this pattern came if it was raining. Then I would erect the tarp and set up camp under it in exactly the same way. I pitched the tent a hundred or so yards away. In areas where bears are a hazard, I use the tent only as a bedroom.

No, the heart of the camp was my seat in front of the pack, where I sat or lay reading, writing, eating, staring into the fire, gazing up at the trees or the sky, at peace with a world where there was no need to do anything but put more wood on the fire. No telephones, no news, no people, no sounds but the wind in the trees, the hum of insects, the call of birds, and the occasional harsh chatter of a squirrel.

The uneventful hiking on the good track continued next morning as the sun came out, disappeared behind dark clouds that hinted at rain, then reappeared. Below ran Walhalla Creek, a rushing stream brown with runoff. A red-tailed hawk soaring high above was the only visible wildlife, though the tracks of moose, bear, elk, and lynx showed that much was hidden. To the south the rounded brown slopes of bare-topped 4,551-foot Pyroxene Mountain dominated the view. In places the forest showed the signs of a big fire, with hundreds of square yards of dead black trees, many still bearing brown, dry needles.

Although still far from the Klondike itself, I was entering the gold-mining area of the Yukon. Pelly River was one of the first to be panned, with the first prospectors arriving in 1883. Ernest Scroggie of Quebec and other prospectors found gold in Scroggie Creek in 1889, and a prospector named LeBoef found gold in Walhalla Creek in 1912. Walhalla was named after the goldfields of Walhalla in Victoria, Australia.

Gold is still mined from the Scroggie Creek gravels today. I wanted, indeed needed, to meet the modern prospectors, as I hoped they would take me over the Stewart River. The Stewart was also a gold-bearing stream where rich finds had been made in 1885, enough for a hundred prospectors to be working there a year later.

Eventually I reached a wider valley with several bulldozed side roads leading off the main track that I worked out should be the one to Scroggie Creek. I camped on a site similar to the one I had left that morning. Thickening clouds to the southwest looked threatening, so I pitched the tarp back in the trees, ready for a quick retreat from my exposed camp if rain fell. Again I was plagued by clouds of blackflies.

I didn't know exactly how far I was from the Stewart River, but knew I should reach it the next day. I was back on a map again, but working out precise positions on a 1:250,000 scale was difficult. Provided I could easily find a lift over the river, Dawson was five days away at most. The sooner I could finish this rather monotonous forested section of the walk, the more time I would have to spend in the more interesting terrain of the Ogilvie Mountains north of Dawson. Perusing the maps, I found the names more interesting than the scenery. Maisy May Creek, Black Hills Creek, Wounded Moose Dome, Tenderfoot Creek, Australia Creek, Eureka Dome,

Bismark Creek, Rob Roy Creek, Too Much Gold Creek. What stories of adventure and hardship lay behind these foreign names, brought into the region by prospectors seeking gold and pioneers looking for a home far from the towns and countries of their birth?

For the first time on the walk I slept badly; weird, half-waking dreams kept me on the verge of consciousness. My head felt tight and my nose was blocked. Raising my pillow of clothes helped, and eventually I fell into a deeper sleep, to be woken by bright sunlight. Within an hour the sky was a sheet of gray and I had packed up the tent and moved under the tarp. The stove spluttered on lighting and went out, just when I felt desperate for a hot drink. I had already used this field-maintainable MSR model for four months on my Canadian Rockies walk, so I knew it well and soon worked out the problem. The washer on the pump that pressurized the fuel tank had dried out and there wasn't enough pressure to vaporize the fuel. Once I'd changed the washer, the stove roared into life. Soon after downing my first mug of coffee I too came, rather sluggishly, to life.

The green hills and the brown creek rolled on. High on the far side of the valley were the white scar and pale buildings of a large mining camp, the first of many I would see during the next week, but there was no sign of activity. The sky remained cloudy but the rain held off. Beside the creek aspen, willow, and wild rose leaves were turning yellow even though it was not yet August. After twenty miles or so the valley flattened out and the wide, gray waters of the Stewart River came into view. I approached it nervously. If I were as alone as I felt, I had a serious problem.

The Stewart is one of the main waterways in the Yukon and was once an important thoroughfare. It was named for James Green Stewart of Montreal. In the winter of 1849 in search of Indians on the orders of Robert Campbell at Fort Selkirk, Stewart had crossed the frozen river, which was previously unknown to the fur traders. The Indians, who knew it well, of course, called it Na Chon-De. The miners nicknamed it the Grubstake River, as it would always provide enough gold to finance a season's prospecting, though never enough to make anyone rich. In 1886 Frederick Harper built a trading post at the mouth of the Stewart, and a NWMP post was established there during the gold rush. The settlement became important again during the 1940s when silver from mines in Mayo, Kena, and Elsa, far to the east, was regularly shipped downriver. Like other riverside settlements, it rapidly faded into insignificance with the coming of the highways. It is still inhabited, though, and as I headed down to the river's edge, the possibility of having to bushwhack the twenty miles there to get a lift over the river was in the back of my mind.

I settled down on a large sandbank beside a bundle of dead trees washed down by the river. They provided a backrest as well as wood for a fire and, potentially, a support for the tarp if it rained. After the closed-in forest camps of the previous few nights, I enjoyed the spacious view up and down the Stewart. There were no signs of any other human visitors.

Finding clean water was a problem; the edge of the river was murky brown from the silt-laden Scroggie Creek inflow. I explored downstream a way but found no clearer water, just fresh bear tracks in the mud less than a quarter mile from my camp. Not wanting to drink muddy water, I donned my already wet boots over bare feet and waded across the mouth of the Scroggie to the clearer water upstream. I boiled the water, knowing there were habitations upstream where the Klondike Highway crossed the Stewart, even though they lay tens of miles away.

I had felt tired all day, with a bad headache, which I put down to the disturbed sleep of the previous night. I continued to feel sick in camp and had no appetite, dumping most of my dinner into the fire. I avoided any thought that I might be ill.

Frequently during the walk I'd heard the strange nasal whir of nighthawks flying around my camps, but I had never seen them. At the Stewart River camp these large, swallowlike birds appeared, and I watched as they swooped and dipped over the river in search of insects as the sky behind them slowly turned pink.

Another restless night ensued. I woke in the dark at two o'clock, soaked in sweat, to what sounded like a rubber ball being squeezed high in the air. What bird made that harsh squawk I had no idea, and I felt too ill to look out to see.

Having arrived at the Stewart River in early evening, I had put aside thoughts of how I would cross it until the next day. The walk had come to a halt; I would stay there until I found someone to ferry me across. Not far downstream was Barker Creek, where I'd been told a prospector was at work. This was confirmed when I came upon a large cleared space in the dense forest that lined the bank. A dirt road led back into the trees, and a bulldozer and a Toyota pickup were parked by the river. A small log cabin stood nearby. Farther along the riverbank stood a larger cabin, ruined and overgrown and marked Barker Creek Placer Mining. A rough track led a couple of hundred yards farther to a sandy beach and a small metal boat that looked recently used. I found fresh bootprints nearby. Following a wide track into the forest a short way, I found no evidence of recent use and decided to wait by the river. Whoever was working here seemed to be away.

I lit a big driftwood fire on the beach, something I had been advised to do as a sure way to attract attention. Then I settled down near the boat to wait, watching the river as it slid past, silent and serene. All around grew sweet ripe raspberries that I nibbled as I scanned the water for any sign of a boat. It seemed strange to be sitting in the middle of this vast, empty wilderness, wondering if or when someone would turn up.

I had just put a pan of water on the fire for coffee when I heard a faint hum. I thought at first it was a plane but soon spotted a riverboat loaded with timber and oil drums. It was surprisingly close and soon swept past me. I jumped up and waved. Someone waved back. I followed the boat's passage upriver to see if it turned in where the vehicles were. It did. I hastily packed up my gear and half walked, half jogged down the track, arriving just as the last drums were being rolled onto the beach.

Two sunburned men stood on the deck staring suspiciously at me. I offered to help. "No thanks," said one abruptly. He had a thick black beard and wore faded blue jeans, a denim shirt, and a leather cowboy hat. "Where've you come from?" he asked. I explained and was given the boat's rope to hold while they finished unloading. They agreed to take me across. "We got a hitchhiker," said his partner, whose beard was fair. Neither was very talkative, and while they weren't unfriendly, I had the strong impression that questions about what they were doing would not be welcome. I needed a lift, so I kept quiet and resisted the strong temptation to take photographs. Sprite, their black Labrador, was much more cheerful. The men kicked the logs they were using as rollers into the river afterward. Sprite dived in and chased them downstream, rounding up the lot and ferrying them in to the bank.

The flat-bottomed utilitarian workboat had a tiny cabin at the rear and two large outboard motors. Once the unloading was finished, I clambered aboard and was taken directly to the far bank. The river, said one of the men, was very low and they'd had problems downstream despite the boat's shallow draft. Maybe I could have forded it after all.

I had first spotted the boat at 3:50 P.M. At 4:30 I stepped ashore on the other side of the river, the major problem of this part of the walk over. I had waited just four hours for a lift. I watched the boat disappear upriver and was alone again in the forest. I set off up the bank, the strange interlude already seeming unreal. Had there really been a boat, two men, a lift? Well, I was across the river, so there must have been.

A forty-five-minute bushwhack through dense, steep forest above some cliffs gave me a taste of what it probably would have been like to follow the Yukon River. I had to make my way back to where the track met the river, but when I found it again the going didn't improve much. In places the track was hard to locate, and I was forced into bushwhacking, including a nasty scramble up a steep gully and a slosh through a mosquito-ridden swamp.

Just before Maisy May Creek, where I intended to camp, I came upon a cabin. Poking about inside among the scattered, mouse-gnawed contents, I found a 1988 calendar and a Hammond Innes paperback with a Whitehorse Library sticker. The due date was March 27, 1980.

Maisy May Creek was silt brown but barely ankle deep. On the far side I found neglected overgrown meadows, a locked and impressive two-story house, and a large unlocked cabin. This had to belong to the Christian community I was told about at Fort Selkirk. It was a long time since this retreat had been used. Inside the cabin I found copies of *National Geographic* for May 1979 and February 1980. I "borrowed" one to read that evening, as it had an article about the 1978 K2 expedition by Galen Rowell. Looking at the fine photographs, I longed to be in mountain country again.

I camped in long grass on the edge of a willow thicket well above the river. Feeling shivery on stopping I finally conceded that I had a bad cold and took two pain killers. Again I couldn't finish my evening meal, and I longed for a hot, sweet drink. But I was running out of coffee and lemonade powder and needing to ration what was left. Necessity forcing experimentation, I discovered that the hot-chocolate powder mixed with dried milk and water and drunk cold was quite refreshing. Although a fire would have been welcome, I didn't light one, as there was no way to do so in the meadows without leaving a scar. A soft sunset ended what had been a good day, one that left the way to Dawson City unimpeded. I was relieved at having crossed the Stewart and realized I had been more worried about how I would do so than I had been prepared to admit.

Again I slept badly, partly due to my cold, partly because of the weather. The heat and humidity in the tent were almost unbearable. Outside the mosquitoes hummed incessantly. I thrashed restlessly, desperate for sleep. Then at 3:30 A.M. a huge clap of thunder jolted me wide awake. Heavy rain and a rushing wind followed, then a flash of lightning and another thunderclap.

The wet weather clung on, and I set off in heavy rain through the extensive pastureland and past workshops and stables. This settlement had been an ambitious undertaking. Samuel Henry set up the first ranch in 1897 to provide hay for the horses in the Klondike and Dawson. By 1906 more than a hundred acres were under cultivation. Whether there had been continuous cultivation since I didn't know, but the land was being left to return to the wild.

Low-flying swallows darted over the meadows, snatching insects out of the moist air as I walked through the long grass and back into the trees. Soon the track turned away from the Stewart River and led northward beside Black Hills Creek, named after the Black Hills of South Dakota by prospectors who had been in the 1870s gold rush there. The sky remained dark and somber, though the rain stopped and the temperature rose to seventy degrees.

As I marched up the rough and overgrown track feeling unwell and not paying much attention to my surroundings, a large, dark object several hundred yards ahead caught my eye. I couldn't see it clearly but felt it was an animal rather than a fallen tree. I stopped and reached for my binoculars in my waist pack. My hands closed on thin air and I remembered I'd put the waist pack in my large pack because of the rain. Taking off the pack was a major chore that I was reluctant to do unless absolutely necessary, so I took a few steps forward. The dark shape loomed ahead, immobile, and now that all my attention was fastened on it, it seemed to grow with every step. Slowly, as I approached, an animal began to take shape, not a grizzly as I feared but a huge bull moose with massive antlers—less worrisome than a bear but still potentially dangerous. The moose stared at me for a few seconds, then turned and trotted off with that high-stepping gait peculiar to the species. This was only the second moose I'd seen on the walk, the other being the one that had awakened me at Lindeman Camp on the Chilkoot Trail five weeks, many miles, and an eon of experience ago.

The previous night I had worked out a route from the Stewart River that would see me in Dawson City in four days. But I hadn't taken my cold into account. My proposed camp this first day was at

Minton Creek, a tributary of Black Hills Creek. But I felt so tired and ill that when I reached McCrimmon Creek, a couple of miles short of Minton, I stopped at a good campsite right by the track. I'd make up the difference the next day, I told myself.

Near the site stood ruined cabins, with garbage and old bits of mining gear strewn everywhere. I had already passed a modern pre-fabricated building with plastic windows ripped apart by animals, and rubbish spread for hundreds of yards all around it. A calendar dated March 1990 suggested it had been recently abandoned. This was my first taste of the lack of respect for the environment shown by many mining concerns, an attitude that soon killed any romantic notions I still harbored about gold prospecting. From the scattered trash I rescued a book on the subject, *Yukon Gold: A Guide for the Modern Goldseeker* by Samuel D. Holloway, which looked like it might contain useful information. I did not intend to look for gold, but I did want to have some understanding of what I saw and what is happening in the Klondike and other areas of the Yukon today.

Rain still threatened, so I slung the tarp between two trees and lit a fire in front of it, burning some of the cut wood that littered the area. I pitched the tent out in the open on a flat, slightly damp spot near the creek. I was hungry and ate a full meal plus a bowl of soup, a sign, I hoped, that I was recovering. Dawson lay sixty or so miles away and I still intended to be there in three days.

The overnight low was just thirty-nine degrees Fahrenheit, making this the coldest night in over a month. It felt very cold too, probably because I was unwell, and for the first time I pulled tight the insulated draft collar on my sleeping bag. Before breakfast I checked my pulse. It was an alarming sixty-eight beats per minute—alarming because five days earlier it had been forty-eight. I still felt ill and a little sorry for myself. Some inspiring scenery to look forward to would have boosted my morale, but I knew that soggy forests and abandoned mining camps were all that lay ahead. Beyond Dawson is the Tombstone Range, I told myself, and you'll be there in a few days if you keep going.

I kept going. A cold west wind helped. In forty minutes I was at Minto Creek, which was dry, so I was glad I had stopped early the night before. Then I came upon a gravel road, lines of spoil heaps, and an abandoned mining camp that I later learned was called Queenstake. Vast amounts of debris lay everywhere, no apparent attempt having been made to clean up the area. Soon I heard the sound of machinery; coming out of the trees onto a high bluff, I found myself looking down on a working mine. The whole valley bottom had been flattened and denuded of vegetation. Dump trucks, looking like toys from this distance, shifted mounds of gravel. I stayed above the noise and the clouds of dust, traversing high on the side of the valley on one of the many gravel roads that laced the area, hoping it would eventually link up with the continuation of the old track obliterated by the mining operations.

Unfortunately it didn't, and at 6:00 P.M. I was back where I had been three hours earlier. The road I had chosen descended to a dead end at a creek. I had cast around in vain for another track. The only alternative to retracing my steps was the even less attractive choice of bushwhacking, so back up I went. The map showed that the main mine road would eventually take me to Dawson City but by a much longer route than the track. There seemed no choice but to follow the road and hope I could regain the more direct route at some point.

A long, long haul up the road took me onto the crest of the hills at thirty-five hundred feet. A pickup stopped and the young woman driving asked me in astonishment what I was doing. She shook her head in disbelief. She had just driven from Whitehorse, which she said was tiring enough. Walking she just couldn't imagine.

Once the road leveled out I was able to appreciate the wide-ranging views and sense of space, very welcome after the days spent in forested valleys. Rolling rounded hills, some wooded, some bare-topped, stretched to the horizon. The sky was overcast and the north wind bitterly cold. Places to camp were plentiful, but water was not. The map suggested I would have to walk many more miles before I'd find any, but I could see two slight dips in the road ahead that marked the heads of shallow valleys leading down to Eureka Creek. At the first dip I left my pack and, containers in hand, headed down into the boggy forest in search of water. If there was any I knew it would collect in this dip. Finding none I returned to the road and went on to the second dip, where I was rewarded by a tiny pool under a seep in the moss about 150 feet down the hillside.

Back on the ridge I pitched the tarp between two small stunted spruces in case of rain and was looking for a tent site when a pickup pulled up. The two people inside were from the Caribou Mine in the next valley and were going to visit friends at Paydirt, the mine I had already passed. They, too, expressed astonishment at meeting a walker. When I said I was from Britain, one of them remembered the article in the *Yukon News*. "If you pass by Caribou," she said, "make sure you drop in for a coffee and a meal."

I hadn't rested or eaten for hours and my head was still stuffy. As I talked I began to feel faint. Not wishing to collapse (it would hardly have fitted my image as a wilderness adventurer!) I ended the conversation and went to lie down. After a few minutes I felt well enough to make broccoli soup and coffee, but I was too tired to bother with a full hot meal, instead just munching two high-calorie MealPack bars. I had felt tense, tired, and chilly on stopping. As I sat under the tarp I began to relax and warm up, though I still felt exhausted. I couldn't collapse until I'd pitched the tent, which took great effort. Afterward I treated myself to a last hot mugful of lemonade. Finally I crawled into the sleeping bag. It had been a long day—ten and a half hours of walking, three of them on a fruit-less side venture. My guess was that I had progressed about fifteen miles. Reaching Dawson City in two days seemed unlikely, espe-cially as I was no longer on my planned route and my cold didn't seem to be clearing up after all.

I woke during the night with throbbing head, soaked in sweat. Much later, I got up to a dull day with clouds covering the tops of the hills. My pulse was still sixty-eight. The sleeping bag was in desperate need of a long airing in the sun, as the down filling was very damp with sweat. "At the moment a day in a hotel with a TV and a bathroom with hot water plus groceries—bread, cheese, salad, fruit juice—and newspapers sounds very appealing!" I wrote in my journal over breakfast.

An hour and a half's walking brought me to a good cut track leading off the gravel road toward Montana Creek. I followed it into the valley bottom and picked up an old, rough track that I hoped was the continuation of the one I had been on before the mining camps intervened. Two trucks were parked at the junction of the tracks and many bootprints led down the valley.

These led to another mining camp that was a total contrast to the larger operations I had seen. A small bulldozer was excavating an old spoil heap and dumping the gravel into the top of a sluice, washed by a jet of water. Just two men were performing this operation. Across the creek was a tent and a large open-sided tarp shelter with a small woodstove inside. A young blond woman stood nearby. A pit bull terrier rushed toward me as I stepped out of the shelter of the trees. He was perfectly friendly, though, and just wanted me to throw sticks for him. "Go on over to the cook tent and grab a coffee. We'll join you soon," shouted one of the men above the noise of the sluice. I nodded and went on. "Would you like some food?" asked the woman, "I'm just cooking up lunch for the boys."

Sitting with a mug of coffee and a plate of spaghetti, I listened as Gail told me about the camp. She made it clear that she wasn't interested in mining but in setting up a self-sufficient farm on the eleven miles of land they owned along Montana Creek. "The Canadian economy's heading for a crash," she said. "Independence is the only way." Charlie and Tom came over. "We're prospecting, not mining," said Charlie. "We leave that to others." This was an old mining area, first staked in 1897 by miners from Montana (hence the name), but they hoped to find gold in the spoil heaps. If they found very much they would bring in a bigger company to mine it, they said. "This is probably the smallest operation in the

Yukon." They were there, I felt, in the spirit of Robert Service, who wrote in "The Spell of the Yukon":

> There's gold and it's haunting and haunting;
> It's luring me on as of old;
> Yet it isn't the gold that I'm wanting
> So much as just finding the gold.

Before I left, Charlie filmed me with his video camera—"I use it as a diary"—while he asked me about my walk and showed me their fridge, a cavity cut into the permafrost just below the thick, wet layer of moss and rotting vegetation that miners call muck.

Clutching gifts of carrots, bananas, apples, oranges, and a lemon, I left after two hours of coffee and conversation. The prospectors were friendly and welcoming, and I had enjoyed their company, but their attitude toward the environment and the wildlife disturbed me. Twice their camp had been raided by black bears and most of their food stolen. They shot one of the bears; its discarded corpse lay in the bushes nearby. They then hung a honey-slathered can of ether from a branch in the hope that the other bear would bite into it and be killed. Instead the bear licked off the honey and then left a pile of dung under the can. Good for the bear, I thought.

The reason they had trouble with bears was that they left their food unprotected in the open cook shelter when they were away, often for several days at a time. It was entirely predictable that the bears would raid camps when there were no people around, yet they seemed to believe that it was easier to kill the bears than to do anything to protect supplies. Bears were seen as vermin rather than magnificent wild animals. They were surprised I was walking unarmed and alone. "Lots of grizzlies in the Ogilvies," they said.

It was good news to be told this track would take me to Calder Creek, and then to roads leading to Dawson. I would do a few more miles before camping. Plodding along, fighting off growing fatigue, I saw willow thickets ahead and sensed a change in the terrain. I needed one, as there was no suitable camp in the wet muskeg I had been in since the mining camp. Soon afterward farm buildings appeared in the midst of overgrown meadows. Pushing my way through the waist-high grass, I found they were mostly ruined shells, though one was intact and reasonably presentable inside. Sticky tape on cracks in the windows, coat hangers whittled from sticks, other makeshift repairs, and candle stubs showed that others had used it since the farm was abandoned. I would do the same. Magazines dating from 1975–77 lay on the table, but there was also a *Yukon News* from June 1988. A child's room upstairs contained a few abandoned toys and a small bed. What, I wondered, had caused the residents to leave their wilderness home. Loneliness, the long, cold, dark winters, crop failures? Had they been glad to go or sad?

An advantage of staying in the farmhouse was that it had a big woodstove that I stoked up so it was pouring out heat—not for me but for my damp sleeping bag, which I hung on a line above the glowing stove. The room became so hot that I decided to sleep in the next one where it was cooler.

But first I needed water. I had figured out I was in the Indian River valley but that the river was at least a mile away. I set off toward it as dusk fell. I was in the middle of the extensive meadows when I suddenly had the feeling I was being watched. I stopped, looked toward the forest, and froze with a mixture of awe, excitement, and fear. A few hundred yards away on the edge of the forest a pack of wolves was watching me. I counted six, some of them pale gray, others almost black. After a few seconds they began to move off slowly, one of them always stationary, watching. When that one fell to the rear of the line, another would stop and the pack would continue on. Eventually they disappeared and I discovered I was holding my breath, and all my muscles were tense. It was less than a month since I'd read Jack London's *White Fang,* which starts with a pack of wolves hunting down two men, and the graphic description of the chase and the kill came unbidden to my mind. But I knew that wolves don't actually regard humans as prey and I was thrilled with this encounter. I had only heard wolves before; seeing them restored a sense of wilderness to an area that seemed ruined by miners.

I found a large pond and filled my water containers. Back in the house I suddenly felt exhausted and dazed. I sat for a few minutes, my head throbbing, then set about making supper. Outside, the wolves howled. I was pushing myself too hard, I decided, given that I wasn't well. I carried the debate into my journal: "Tomorrow I shall get as far as I comfortably can but not push for Dawson. An extra half day doesn't matter and means I'll arrive feeling fairly fresh. Driving myself into the ground is pointless." I sliced my precious lemon in two, squeezed the juice into my mug, and added hot water and sugar. It tasted delicious, a vast improvement over lemonade powder.

For once I had an undisturbed night, though I still woke with a thick head. It had been raining when I fell asleep, but now the sun was shining through the windows. Chopped banana made my granola tastier, and the bright sunlight made me feel more like walking than I had for several days.

The Indian River marks the southern boundary of the Klondike goldfields. Between the Indian and the Klondike rivers are the richest gold-bearing creeks. I waded to the promised land that had pulled all those thousands over the Chilkoot Pass in the bitter depths of winter and then down the Yukon River in their ramshackle craft. A mining camp lay on the far side, beside what I guessed was Quartz Creek. Two boys, aged seven or eight, confirmed that it was. They pointed out the decaying remains of a large dredge. "That's No. 7 Dredge," I was told by these nascent tour guides. I picked my way through tailings and old mines for a time until I came on a gravel road that led to the junction with Calder Creek, a smaller stream that I followed upward on an overgrown bulldozed track.

Quartz Creek is important in the history of the Klondike because it was here in the winter of 1893–94 that William Redford discovered the first gold in the area (although Robert Henderson, the first to find gold in a tributary stream of the Klondike River, is often given credit), proving incorrect the prevailing view that none would be found in the area. The find soon brought other prospectors, and the scene was set for the big strike that would spark the gold rush. Redford himself stayed on Quartz Creek despite the much richer finds elsewhere, working there every year until 1937, making a living though never a fortune.

The divide between Calder and Eldorado creeks is where the "public" part of the Klondike starts. Once down by Eldorado I knew there would be traffic, working mines, and tourist attractions but probably nowhere quiet and private to camp. The lack of water, however, prevented me from camping on the divide, even though it seemed an otherwise excellent site and I was again very tired. A good gravel road led toward Eldorado Creek. Five minutes down the road I found a seep of water, I filled my bottles, and returned to the divide. The rain that had hung about all afternoon cleared to a fine sunny evening and good views down the wide, straight valley of Eldorado Creek. Dawson lay some fifteen miles away, all downhill or on the level and on good roads. An early start would see me there in time for lunch.

I woke at five, again soaked in sweat, having already woken earlier with a headache. My sodden sleeping bag prompted me to get up. The sky was clear and the temperature forty-six degrees.

I was down in the valley before the first tourists arrived, but it was soon clear that it is they who are mined for gold now. The Eldorado and Bonanza Creek valleys present the romantic face of gold mining, the image of the tough prospector fighting the elements and searching for gold with just a pan and shovel. The destruction, waste, and pollution is hidden. There are vast spoil heaps, of course, and restored dredges for the visitors to ogle, but they are shrouded with the cloak of history that makes all things acceptable.

I trudged down the road reading the many plaques telling tales of amazing gold strikes and the larger-than-life characters who had made them. The most important of these markers is the Discovery Monument, which commemorates the spot on Bonanza Creek where in August 1896 George Carmacks and his Indian companions, Skookum Jim and Tagish Charlie, discovered gold and precipitated the Klondike gold rush that would lead to the creation of the Yukon Territory. Gold had been found in the area before but never enough to interest anyone but the dedicated, hard-bitten men to whom prospecting was a way of life. The find on Bonanza Creek (known as Rabbit Creek before the strike but renamed by Carmacks) changed all that, inspiring thousands who had no knowledge of prospecting—who had never even considered gold seeking before—to head for this remote, inhospitable region. By 1911 well over 140 million Canadian dollars of gold had been taken from the Klondike streams, though few of the stampeders saw any of it. Long before they reached the Klondike all the worthwhile claims had been staked.

Enough prospectors were working the streams in the area by 1896 to ensure that eventually a big strike would be made. The sense of an impending strike had been mounting since the experienced but not very successful prospector named Robert Henderson had found gold on a tributary of the Klondike River that he called Gold Bottom Creek. Soon afterward Henderson met Carmacks beside the Klondike River and invited him to stake a claim on Gold Bottom. Exhibiting the prejudice against Indians then common, he also told Carmacks that the offer wasn't open to "damn Siwashes" (Siwash was an insulting term for the Indians). After Henderson had gone Carmacks told Skookum Jim that they would find a creek of their own. They did—Rabbit Creek. Although they let Henderson know they were prospecting there, they didn't tell him when they made the big strike, and he worked on in ignorance just on the other side of the hill as the gold rush started. His racism may well have cost him a fortune. Luck was not with him even on Gold Bottom: the main strike was made on another claim.

Henderson always maintained that he was the real discoverer of the Klondike gold, and eventually the Canadian government recognized him as codiscoverer with Carmacks. Still seeking the big strike that forever eluded him, Henderson carried on prospecting throughout the Yukon and British Columbia right up to his death in 1933.

The three men who launched the gold rush were not typical prospectors. George Washington Carmacks had arrived in the Yukon via the Chilkoot Pass in 1885; although ostensibly there to look for gold, he was more interested in the Tagish Indians whose lifestyle he adopted. He married the daughter of a chief and worked with the Indians, packing goods over the Chilkoot. In 1893 he found coal near Five Finger Rapids on the Yukon River and built a cabin nearby on the site of the settlement that today bears his name. The other white men in the area regarded him as a renegade, giving him the derogatory nicknames Squaw Man and Siwash George, but in fact Carmacks was intelligent and well educated. He had an organ and many works of classical literature in his cabin near Five Finger Rapids; he wrote poetry and subscribed to various learned journals, including *Scientific American*.

When Henderson met him at the mouth of the Klondike River, Carmacks was fishing with the aim of selling the salmon he caught as dog food. His initial interest in the Rabbit Creek area was centered on logs, not gold. Indeed, it seems likely that his Indian companions, the brothers of his wife, Kate, were more interested in finding gold than he was.

Skookum Jim Mason was noted for his strength, having packed a record 156 pounds of bacon over the Chilkoot Pass. He was also keen to be a successful prospector and was later to claim that he rather than Carmacks found the first nugget of gold in Rabbit Creek. Regardless of who was first, both Skookum Jim and Tagish Charlie registered claims on the creek and became rich men, rich enough to be regarded as white men by society at the time. Despite his mining royalties of ninety thousand dollars a year,

Skookum Jim carried on prospecting without rest until he died, worn out from his labors, in 1916. Tagish Charlie, who was known as Dawson Charlie after the strike, became the first Yukon Indian to be made a full Canadian citizen. He sold his claim and opened a hotel in Carcross, which he ran until 1908 when he fell from the railway bridge in Carcross and drowned. Carmacks moved to Vancouver, British Columbia, where he lived comfortably until his death in 1922 at the age of sixty-two.

Most of the claims on the creeks are sifted over by their current owners from time to time for the last scraps of gold, though it seems that the bulk of the gold has been taken out. There is one claim, run by the Klondike Visitors Association, at Grand Forks where Eldorado and Bonanza creeks meet, where visitors can try their hand at panning for gold for free. Klondike gold is placer gold, that is gold that has been washed down watercourses to settle in the gravel of the sandbars (placer comes from the Spanish for sandbank, *placel*) and creek beds where traces of it, known as color, can be found by panning. Many people think that panning is the way the gold is mined. Actually, it's just a way of finding out whether a section of creek has gold in it and is worth mining properly. Mining is digging down to the bedrock and sifting through the gravel by means of sluices and, in big operations, dredges.

If you want to be certain of finding gold, you can pay to pan in a spiked, wooden imitation sluice at Claim 33. I was more interested in the snacks served in the souvenir shop and in relaxing with a cup of coffee at a picnic table. I watched a burly man in a Greenpeace T-shirt videotaping the area, the only other person about as it was still early. He came over and said, "Hi, I'm Pat Murphy from Alaska and I'm making a video for Yukon Tourism. Would you like to be in it?" I agreed to be filmed taking off my pack and sitting down at a table and then picking it up and walking away. He recruited one of the staff from the shop to be filmed panning for gold. Pat told me he made his living by photographing Alaska and the Yukon, with both still and video cameras, and that he spent as much time as possible in the wilderness. We had much in common, and I enjoyed our talk but soon felt I wanted to push on. Dawson was now tantalizingly near.

By the time I reached Dawson I was footsore and my head was aching again. I had intended to pitch the tent on the campground and to stay only one day, but now I felt that if I was to shake off this cold and be fit for the rest of the walk I needed a few days' rest in a hotel. My sleeping bag desperately needed drying out too, so I headed for the center of town and the Triple J Hotel. I checked in for three nights, even though it cost ninety dollars a night. A huge meal in the restaurant and a hot bath followed. The post office held a mass of mail from friends, some of which contained news I could have done without.

Back home my precarious finances were being handled by a good friend, Denise Thorn. A letter from her informed me starkly that some book royalties were far less than I had expected because, it turned out, of my failure to understand the fine print of my contract regarding overseas sales. As I digested this information, I read the next line. A magazine for which I wrote regularly would not be paying me over the summer and would probably have to cease publication. This was a double blow, as I was also an unpaid nonexecutive director of the company that published the magazine. I resolved on the spot never to get involved in business again. I was living on a bank overdraft that Denise had negotiated and would have to keep my expenses as low as possible. I thought of my ninety-dollar-a-night room and was glad I had booked in before I collected my mail. The news left me worried and agitated. It didn't help that I was still feeling ill.

Although it seemed a crazy thing to do, I phoned Denise in Scotland. She was expecting the call. "Things aren't that bad," she reassured me, "and it's important you finish the walk." I did need to hear that. The situation was bad, but I couldn't do anything about it immediately, and abandoning the walk wouldn't help. Apart from letting down my sponsors, quitting would have left me feeling defeated. I needed to consider how I could minimize my expenditures for the rest of the walk so I could finish the trip.

My original aim had been to walk to the northern edge of the Yukon on the Beaufort Sea if the weather permitted. To do so would mean arranging an expensive flight back by bush plane and possibly an air drop of food as well. My second choice had been to finish by leaving the Yukon across its northeast border with the Northwest Territories. This now looked like the only option regardless of the weather, as I couldn't afford the cost of the flights.

The Dawson Tourist office held my supplies and a note from George Sinfield that said two boxes had gone north on a Gold City Tours coach to be dropped on the Dempster Highway at the highway maintenance camps at Ogilvie River and Eagle Plains. On my second day in Dawson I dropped in to the Gold City Tours office to thank the boss, Buffalo Taylor, who sported a glorious handlebar mustache, for sending on my supplies. "They left this very morning," he said. "Did you see George?" He had been in Dawson the day I arrived, it turned out, staying in his van in the RV park. I had missed him again.

My supplies contained a down pullover, thick thermal sweater, pile mitts, gaiters, and three new pairs of thick wool socks. My pack was going to be heavier from here on, but I would be prepared for the winter everyone told me was about to begin. In Dawson's stores I bought stove fuel, stainless steel spoons to replace my cracked and broken plastic ones, and maps I hadn't been able to find in Whitehorse. I had some surplus food I sold for twenty-five dollars to one of the stores. I needed every penny I could get.

I stayed three full days in Dawson, not wanting to leave until I felt fully fit. The town itself has much of interest for the visitor. Founded in 1896 where the Klondike River runs into the Yukon, the only suitable site for a large settlement near the goldfields, it was the capital of the Yukon from 1897 to 1951. In its heyday during the gold rush, it housed five thousand people and serviced thirty thousand more, and was the largest city north of San Francisco and west of Winnipeg. It was named for Dr. George Dawson, director of the Geological and Natural History Survey of Canada.

George Dawson led the first geological survey of the Yukon Territory in 1887, seventeen years after Canada bought the territory from the Hudson's Bay Company. The expedition was in part a response to Schwatka's earlier U.S. Army expedition. Despite being in permanent poor health from a childhood illness, Dawson traveled a tough route from Wrangell on the Alaskan coast up the Stikine and Liard rivers and then down the Pelly to the Yukon. He then went up the Yukon to its headwaters and finally back to the coast over the Chilkoot Pass, which his partner William Ogilvie had earlier crossed in the other direction. (George Carmacks, Skookum Jim, and Tagish Charlie were among Ogilvie's packers.) Ogilvie went on to survey the Alaska-Yukon border in the Fortymile region. In 1896 he made the first surveys of the Klondike and the Dawson City town site. Between 1898 and 1901 he was the commissioner of the Yukon Territory. His name was given to the Ogilvie River in the northern Yukon in 1888 and then to the Ogilvie Mountains in 1966.

Today just sixteen hundred people live in Dawson City year-round, and the main trade is tourism rather than gold, though it is the romance of the Klondike that brings the visitors. With that in mind Dawson has been restored to look as much as possible as it did in the late 1890s, with wooden boardwalks and dusty, unpaved streets. Many of the buildings have been renovated in the original style too, and you can still gamble in Diamond Tooth Gertie's Gambling Hall or watch the Gaslight Follies variety show in the old Palace Grand Theatre.

The cabin where Robert Service lived and wrote many of his poems is open to visitors, and there are daily readings of his best-known verses. He didn't actually reach the Yukon or write any poems about the area until 1904, and several more years passed before he moved to Dawson City, where he worked as a bank clerk until his poems began to make money. Before that Service, who was born in England and brought up in his father's native Scotland, had wandered up and down the Pacific coast of the United States and Canada for six years after his arrival in Canada in 1896, doing a variety of casual labor before starting work in a bank in Vancouver. From there he was transferred to Whitehorse and then to Dawson. He was enthralled with the romance of the American West and the gold rush, and carried his feelings into his poetry, which is in large part responsible for the fame and the myths of the Yukon and the Klondike. Service had a genuine love of the northern wilderness and spent much time on solo walks and canoe trips. He wrote novels as well as poetry, and his *Trail of '98* is a realistic reconstruction of the gold-rush days. Service only spent nine of his eighty-four years (he died in 1958) in the Yukon, but these are the ones for which he is remembered.

Unlike Robert Service, Jack London did take part in the gold rush, crossing the Chilkoot Pass in the fall of 1897. He didn't find any gold, though, and he didn't stay long. However, his experiences were enough to inspire a series of writings about the north, of which the best known is *The Call of the Wild*. There is also a London cabin in Dawson, but it is a reconstruction, the original having been on Henderson Creek where London prospected. Parts of the original cabin are incorporated into the replica, the rest being part of an identical replica in Jack London Square in Oakland, California. The story of finding the cabin is told in an interesting pamphlet entitled *Jack London's Cabin,* by Dick North, who runs the Jack London Interpretive Centre in Dawson.

To cater to its visitors, Dawson has many cafés and restaurants. After three weeks eating mostly dried trail food, I thoroughly enjoyed every one. My favorite was Nancy's on the waterfront, which served some of the best pizza I've ever had. I also washed and repaired my gear, read several books, and tried to relax. By the fourth morning I was restless and ready to move on. My pulse was down to fifty-two and all trace of my cold had gone. Ahead lay the spectacular mountains of the Tombstone Range and beyond them the Arctic. There was still much to do and see.

7

Return to the Mountains: The Tombstone Range

DAWSON CITY TO TOMBSTONE

RECREATIONAL PARK

AUGUST 7–14, 66 MILES

Though hardships and perhaps
dangers were encountered, the great
wonderland made compensation
beyond our most extravagant hopes.

—John Muir, *Travels in
Alaska*

From the steep cut in the forest Dawson looked small and insignificant, overshadowed by the waves of wooded hills fading into the sky and the twisting silver thread of the Yukon River disappearing to the right and left. Pausing frequently to look back at the diminishing checkerboard of the town, I slogged straight up Midnight Dome, the hill that towers above Dawson.

Midnight Dome was originally called Moosehide Hill for the shape and brownish red color of a large rock slide visible on the Dawson side. Around 1900, people began climbing the hill to watch the midsummer sun setting and rising almost simultaneously. Soon this midnight picnic became an annual event and the hill became known by the rather more romantic name of Midnight Dome.

On the summit I came upon a fire tower, a very necessary feature, as Dawson is surrounded by forests and fires are common. Indeed, in the early years of the town much of it burned down on several occasions. The site of the tower, twenty-four hundred feet above Dawson, gave excellent views of the Klondike hills and the Yukon River. I watched the river for a long time. It had been an important feature in my life for the past six weeks and I would not see it again. Finally, I turned my back on the great river and looked north to the long, distant line of the jagged, exciting peaks of the Tombstone Range, the southernmost summits of the Ogilvie Mountains. It was time to move on, both physically and mentally, for the walk was changing and I would have to change with it.

"Good view isn't it?" said a voice. "But there'll be rain soon." A big man who moved quietly was standing close behind me. Bill Jackson, the fire ranger, resided in a roomy cabin just back in the bushes from the tower. "Come inside and have a whiskey," he offered as the first drops of rain began to fall from the black storm clouds sweeping in over the trees.

"Where are you from?" Britain, I replied. "Saxon?" asked Bill, unexpectedly. I suppose so, I admitted cautiously, suspecting that this was a loaded question. I was right, and as thunder cracked and lightning flashed outside, Bill launched into a lengthy attack on Saxons and their treacherous nature, a tirade that swept grandly through a rather suspect history from the Romans through King Arthur to the Black and Tans. He was, he told me, of Scots-Irish descent and therefore a Breithon, the correct name for Celts. All English people were Saxons. "You look like a typical Saxon," he said. He assured me that as a Christian he held no animosity to individual Saxons, but he had studied the subject and assured me that history showed Saxons were not to be trusted.

This bizarre monologue, during which I hardly uttered a word, was made even more unreal by the whiskey and the special effects of the storm raging outside. Bill talked unabated for an hour or so and would undoubtedly have continued much longer if the rain hadn't stopped and I hadn't insisted on leaving.

Outside, the air was fresh and sharp. The fire road I had ascended, now a sandy, rutted track that didn't look as though vehicles ever used it, rolled on through the wooded gentle Moosehide Hills. Every so often the enticing Tombstone peaks slipped into view, pulling me on.

I had not left Dawson until early afternoon, and with the time spent at the fire tower, it was midnight when I reached Lepine Creek some sixteen miles later. The area around the slow-flowing stream was boggy and thick with willows, but there was a roughly cleared patch of dryish ground just back from the road and a fresh fire ring on the track itself. I used both. A party with horses had clearly been here not long ago, and I was grateful for their facilities. A full moon rose and a star appeared. It was, I realized, the first real night of the walk, a further sign that the nature of my adventure was changing. Supper was a piece of cold pizza from Nancy's, but despite not needing to cook I didn't retire until 2:00 A.M. Sitting in the dark surrounded by the secretive silence of the night-shrouded forest was a pleasurable and unfamiliar experience.

Lepine Creek is the site of an old sawmill, and there was much rusting machinery lying round. The mill had provided wood to build the flumes that transported water for the Twelve Mile power plant and water system and also fuel for the steam shovels that dug the ditches for the system. The power plant was built between 1906 and 1909 to provide electricity for the large gold dredges that had taken over from pick-and-shovel miners in the Klondike. The system also provided power for hydraulic mining, which requires higher pressure than pumps of the time could provide to wash the gold out of the gravel. More than sixty miles of flumes, ditches, and pipelines were built, a major engineering feat. The system was abandoned in 1925, but many relics can be found in the area.

A day and a half more of the twisting, turning fire road took me to the edge of the mountains and the end of easy walking. The scenery was no more than pleasant, and I walked fast, drawn by the distant mountains. A point of interest was the Ballarat Creek inverted siphon, one of seven pipelines built to carry water to the goldfields across unavoidable depressions with the least height loss. The wooden pipeline itself is long gone, but a line of the iron hoops that once held it together still marks the route. In places the fire road dwindled to a narrow trail recently cleared with an ax, presumably by one of the horse parties that had come this way.

Beyond the fire road I climbed above timberline and walked the glorious ridge above North Rock Pass. Ahead lay mountains, real jagged rock mountains, the first I had set foot in since coming down from Mount Lorne six long weeks earlier. I felt, paradoxically, as though I had come home, yet I was excited at the sight of the unknown kingdom I was about to enter. Exhilarated and inspired, I strode on toward the peaks.

My progress to the heights was abruptly halted in the Little Twelve Mile River valley, which was narrow, steep-sided, and choked with a dense, almost impenetrable tangle of willow and alder thickets. I stumbled and clawed just two miles in two hours. My mood changed from elation to frustration and anger. Bad temper was essential—in fact, nothing less would have kept me going through that jungle. The pack caught repeatedly on branches, my clothes were snagged and torn, I was lathered with sweat, and a cloud of mosquitoes buzzed around my head. This was one occasion on which I was glad to be alone. This trial would surely have brought a falling out with a companion. As it was I was free to shout and swear at the bushes.

A dark line of collapsed decaying wooden boards marked the remains of the Little Twelve Mile flume intake, the start of a long pipeline that took water down to the Twelve Mile power plant and my destination for the day. The climb that lay beyond it would be the morning's challenge. Finding a campsite took time since there was little clear ground and the area available was damp and mossy. Eventually I located a narrow, flat strip of dry, stony ground overhung with willows, probably a dried-up stream channel. I set up my kitchen at one end, the tent at the other, then lit a small fire. The damp willow and alder sticks put out more smoke than heat. I resisted the temptation to burn bits of the intake, feeling that historic artifacts should be left to rot in peace. A halo around the moon suggested that the clear weather would not last.

Steady rain and a slippery, thigh-deep, very cold ford through the white water of Little Twelve Mile River got the next day off to a shivery start. The eighteen-hundred-foot climb that followed, however, soon warmed me up. I cut through steep spruce forest and then head-high willows. A stretch of alpine tundra led to Sheep Pass, one of the few routes across the Tombstone Range that walkers (rather than climbers) can use. North of the pass lay the Tombstone River, which would take me into the heart of the range.

Trying to avoid losing altitude after the pass, I contoured eastward across the talus- and scrub-covered slopes of Sheep Mountain. High above, a pale movement caught my eye. Five Dall sheep, ewes with young, were traversing the rocky mountainside. I wished I were able to move as quickly and easily across the steep terrain. A thought occurred to me: I had now seen caribou on Caribou Mountain and sheep on Sheep Mountain! If there was a Grizzly Peak, I'd give it a miss.

A long, slippery descent on steep, loose rocks led to the Tombstone River valley. Ahead lay the huge piles of disintegrating talus and boulders that make up the Cloudy Range, while slowly coming into view to the east were the smoother granite cliffs and turrets of the Tombstone Range. The rain had stopped and the light was improving rapidly, saturating the land with an unreal poststorm glow.

I had hoped to camp below 7,191-foot Tombstone Mountain itself that night, but after eight hours of difficult walking I was tired and stopped for the day. The previous three days had all been long and arduous. A fourth late night would have left me shattered. This wasn't an area to rush through, anyway, but one to savor, to enter slowly and gently and experience fully.

Prospectors who entered this area in 1897–98 in search of elusive riches named Tombstone Mountain for its appearance. Because they had no maps, this distinctive peak was an important landmark, as it was also to trappers and, later, Mounted Police patrols. Unknown to the prospectors, the peak had already been named Mount Campbell by William Ogilvie in 1896, after the chief factor of the Hudson's Bay Company, Robert Campbell. Campbell had discovered the Pelly and Upper Yukon rivers and built Fort Selkirk. It wasn't until 1968 that it was finally concluded that Mount Campbell and Tombstone Mountain were in fact the same peak and the latter name was officially adopted, though some maps still give it as Mount Campbell.

That night's site, on a little sandy hillock above the Tombstone River with superb views upstream to the black wedge of Tombstone Mountain and the pinnacle-topped wall of Mount Monolith, was the best of the walk so far, though only a faint promise of what was to come.

The next day, I found that walking into this mountain sanctuary was like walking into paradise. As befits the way of a pilgrim, the going was rough, leading gradually through dense brush, across willow-thicketed creeks and over moss-covered, half-hidden boulders into the inner sanctum, the magnificent rock amphitheater that is the Tombstone Range, a huge curving ridge of heart-stopping granite walls and spires. Talus Lake, a boulder-ringed, brooding mountain tarn, backed by a towering cliff that looked about to topple into the water, made my fifth night out from Dawson one of the most magnificent wilderness camps I have ever had. Beyond the rippling waters Tombstone Mountain darkened into blackness as the sky deepened from pink into the dark blue of night.

Perfection is not easy to find. Some would say it is an ideal, a goal to seek but never achieve. Perhaps, most of the time, but I found it at Talus Lake on the morning of August 12, 1990, a morning so beautiful, so faultless that I almost felt guilty for being there, almost wondered what I had done to deserve such rapture. But on reflection I knew what it had taken to immerse myself in the mountain glory granted to me, knew that without the days spent struggling through dense forest, slogging through mud and rain under a heavy load, and plodding along alone with my thoughts I wouldn't have been able to accept what that morning gave me.

Bright light shining on my face through the open door of the tent woke me. The sun had just appeared over the jagged Mount Monolith ridge. The sky was clear and blue, the light cool and sharp as crystal. Across Talus Lake the sun cut across the face of Tombstone Mountain, highlighting the complicated rock architecture, revealing one by one the ridges and faces that rose to the great tapered summit pyramid. Rocks jutting out of the lake shone in the sunshine, tiny imitations of the greater rock that lay beyond them, both reflected in the barely rippling water. I sat by the lake edge and sank into the landscape, feeling simultaneously serene and elated. Silence and stillness seemed the only responses to such overwhelming grandeur, yet inside I was exploding with joyous energy.

I wandered toward broad, flat Tombstone Pass, which at five thousand five hundred feet lay five hundred feet above Talus Lake. Six Dall sheep roamed high on the mountainside below the great north face of Mount Monolith, which was first climbed as recently as 1978. High above towered the inaccessible-looking pinnacle that makes up its summit.

As I was watching the sheep a closer movement caught my eye. I turned in astonishment as a hiker materialized, a thin sun-tanned young man wearing just shorts and blue nylon boots and carrying a tiny day pack. He was the first walker I had seen since leaving Matti and Erkki in Carcross seven weeks earlier. He waved and greeted me in a guttural accent. "From Germany," he said when I asked. He and his companion had taken four days to reach Talus Lake from the Dempster Highway via the upper North Klondike River, a distance of only ten miles. There was no trail in the valley bottom, he told me, and the walking in dense willows and alders was difficult. They had roamed away from the river at times too, though he wasn't sure exactly where they had been, as they only had a 1:250,000 map. Their camp was at Divide Lake, my intended destination, just a couple of miles away,.

His brown skin, hard muscles, and indefinable air of being at home in the wilderness made me ask where else he had been. "Oh, we started with the West Coast Trail near Vancouver," he said casually, "then hitchhiked up to Teslin in the Yukon, where we built a raft and floated down the Yukon River to Dawson." They would have to go home soon, but first they would visit either Kluane or Denali National Park in Alaska, they hadn't yet decided.

We parted, he for Talus Lake, I for lake-dotted Tombstone Pass on the divide between the Tombstone and North Klondike rivers. As I began the gentle descent to Divide Lake, another movement attracted my attention. Away to the north four horses, two with riders, were ascending the valley. The horsemen were too far away to hail, but that evening the German hiker told me he had spoken with them. They were a hunter and a guide in search of bears. It had taken them five hours to make the ascent from the Dempster Highway.

At Divide Lake I found the German hikers' small green single-hoop tent pitched on a nice site beside the trickling outlet creek, the start of the infant North Klondike River. A shiny alcohol-burning Trangia stove was perched on a rock outside. The hiker had asked me what stove I was using, then told me of an English couple they had camped near who had the same model. "It exploded!" he said, making clear what he thought of white-gas stoves. That night at my camp a quarter mile away I checked my stove carefully and lit it with great circumspection. It worked perfectly, as it had and was to do throughout the walk. I spent the rest of the evening watching the mountains sink into darkness and, more prosaically, patching my trousers, which had begun to suffer from the bushwhacking, and wondering which way to go from here.

My intended plan had been to head north through the Cloudy Range and then follow river valleys out to the Dempster, but the distance was seventy-five miles, and now that I had experienced the realities of bushwhacking in this area I knew that could easily mean a week's hard walking. As I had left Dawson with ten days' food and this was my sixth day out, I would clearly have to abandon this plan or go hungry. My next food was, I hoped, at the Ogilvie River highway maintenance camp at Mile 122. If I walked out down the

North Klondike River I would hit the highway at Mile 45. I decided to take an inventory of my supplies and see just how long they would last.

"Something has been at my food!" My journal entry expresses my surprise at finding holes gnawed through the tough nylon of both my food bags. The previous night I had stashed each one separately under bushes at least twenty-five yards from my kitchen site, yet both had been raided by something with sharp teeth. That morning, packing in a serene daze, I had not noticed the damage, the holes being in the base of each bag. I checked through the contents and was relieved to find little had actually disappeared. The thief had bitten into but not consumed a freeze-dried cheese-nut casserole, taken a large chunk out of a compressed fruit-and-nut Pemmican bar, and eaten into a bag of dried figs.

Sorting out my food showed that I had just enough for five days, but if I were out for six I'd be a little hungry. I had more than enough drink materials and books, having not wanted to run out again—not that I was doing much reading. I would, I decided, head for the highway the next day, then follow it, with diversions off to the sides if possible, to my next food drop. Despite the experience of the other hikers, I guessed there must be a trail somewhere in the North Klondike River valley. Otherwise how had the horse party reached here so quickly?

In the morning a delicate dew sparkled on the grasses. The light on the lake and the granite walls was magnificent, cool and gray in the shadows, warm and golden in the sun. Above, the deep blue of the sky spoke of another glorious high-summer day. Enraptured by the beauty and not thinking about what I was doing, I sprinkled lemonade powder instead of dried milk on my granola! It tasted okay if a little odd. I was glad I hadn't put it in my coffee. I finally labeled the identical self-sealing bags.

To avoid the thick bush in the valley bottom, I stayed high for as long as possible, contouring east across talus and light scrub to a wide, sloping, rocky terrace below Rockcandy Mountain, a name I considered corny at best. The views were spacious and superb. Across the dark line of vegetation that marked the river lay the eastern end of the crumbling Cloudy Range, while to the west Tombstone Pass slowly shrank into the distance.

Where the terrace faded into steeper, rougher ground I dropped down into the valley, making use of the many game trails that laced the increasingly thick and tangled undergrowth. Then, to my great and everlasting delight, I found a good pack trail that made the walk through the thick bush fast and easy rather than the nightmare struggle I had expected. The trail took me to within a mile of the highway, finally ending at a wide, shallow, stony section of the North Klondike River up which, I guessed, horse parties waded. Two people lay sunbathing on the bank next to their massive packs. They were German, and I remembered what I'd been told at Fort Selkirk—"the Yukon is famous in Germany." These two backpackers had been in the area for several days and were also heading back to the highway.

I forded the knee-deep river and soon found the trail again on the far side, wide and well used here. I reached the highway after just seven hours and fifteen minutes, several hours sooner than expected.

Knowing the Tombstone Recreational Park campground was located at the highway, I expected to meet people. Even so, I felt strangely resentful when I was hailed by two day hikers before I had even reached the site and dropped my pack. In part I was not yet ready to deal with people who hadn't been in the wilderness, who couldn't, I arrogantly thought, appreciate what I had experienced. But I wasn't misanthropic enough to turn down the invitation of a hot drink, especially as there was something about the people who offered it that attracted me. I dumped my pack at an empty site—one of the few as there were RVs everywhere—and joined them. It was nearly five hours later when I left! By that time I had not only had several hot drinks but also a good supper of thick soup made from ramen noodles and fresh carrots, potatoes, and garlic.

Dawna Rose and Ian Dowle were from Saskatchewan and were traveling the North on motorbikes, camping overnight and taking days off for walks into the wilderness. They were now on the return leg, heading back to Dawson from Inuvik at the northern end of the Dempster Highway. We sat and swapped tales of our adventures in front of a sputtering, smoky campfire.

A sudden flurry of activity among the other campers caught our attention. The word *grizzly* echoed back and forth. One had been seen on the slopes of Outrider Mountain across the highway. Scanning the hillside with my binoculars, I soon picked it up, a large dark bear moving slowly. It was the first of the trip, and I mused on the irony of seeing one now from the safety of a crowded highway campground when I had seen none when I was alone in the bush.

As I was setting up the tent at half past midnight, more muted but excited whispering reached me. I looked up. A mysterious swirl of pale green light decorated the sky briefly before fading into the light of a bright half-moon. Another first for the walk. The glimpse was quite thrilling, as I had seen the northern lights only once before, in Lapland in the European Arctic several years earlier.

At eleven the next evening I was still at the Tombstone Recreational Park. I had spent seven hours talking to Dawna and Ian about everything under the sun from the nature of art—they were both artists and studying painting at the university in Saskatoon—to the nature of travel. It was a pleasant, relaxing way to spend a sunny day. After a week's walking, a day off was welcome. It was strange to remember that these people, friends now, were the same ones whose greeting I had resented only the day before.

During the day I also visited the nature interpretative center in the campground and picked up leaflets on hunting and trapping and the native Indians, something I had wanted to learn more about since my conversations with J. Roger Alfred at Fort Selkirk—the last long conversations I'd had with anybody until now, I realized.

Fur had been the initial incentive for exploring the northern

Yukon, the rich animal life attracting white trappers under the aegis of the Hudson's Bay Company long before any prospectors thought of searching for gold in the creeks to the south. Today hunting and trapping are strictly controlled, the Dempster Highway having opened up the north to exploitation and made it all too easy for irresponsible hunters to annihilate animal populations. Only native hunters, whether Indian or Inuit, are free to hunt without licenses and don't have to report their kills. They have lived in harmony with their land for generations. It is, sadly, white hunters and trappers who kill for trophies to mount on the wall and furs for indulgent fashions. The European movement west into the Yukon was in part the result of overtrapping farther east. Beaver was a prime fur in the nineteenth century for making hats for so-called gentlemen. Later other furs came into fashion. R. M. Patterson, who spent a winter working a trap line in the Nahanni River area of the Mackenzie Mountains in the Northwest Territories, writes in his book *Dangerous River* that trapping is "a cruel business, but one that will endure as long as women wear marten stoles."

Later in the day a middle-aged couple from Whitehorse came over to my camp to talk. Rusty and Bill, it turned out, knew George Sinfield. The fine weather, they told me, was forecast to last at least three or four days more.

The evening was peaceful and quiet. The urge to push on and finish the walk that had dogged me a few days before had completely vanished. Remembering it, I decided that my worries had been caused by the slow progress of bushwhacking. Finding the trail down the North Klondike River valley and having a rest day had banished my concern. I was also pleased at the lack of traffic along the Dempster. As road walks go it should be quite pleasant, I thought.

8

Dodging the Dempster

TOMBSTONE PARK TO EAGLE PLAINS

AUGUST 15–30, 202 MILES

When you have walked for days
under the enormous sky . . . you
begin to sense the timeless,
unsummarized dimensions of a
deeper landscape.

—Barry Lopez, *Arctic
Dreams*

hree breakfasts made for a slow start the next morning. The
first was my usual granola and coffee with the addition of an
orange from Bill. He was back shortly. "Come and have some tea
and toast. We have plenty." As I munched on crunchy wholemeal
toast spread with sweet jam, Bill and Rusty told me they were heading for Inuvik and might stop at Eagle Plains. They would return the
next day. "We want to be back in Dawson in two days because it's
Discovery Day," said Bill, "and the celebrations are really good."
Discovery Day is August 17, the day gold was found on Rabbit
Creek and the day that led to the creation of Dawson City.

Reflecting on the vast difference in the perception of distance
for the traveler on foot and the traveler on wheels, I realized what a
gulf there is between the two modes. To me Eagle Plains was two
weeks away, too far to even think about, while Dawson was a week
behind me. To Bill and Rusty both were less than a day's journey.
The vast and wild land shrinks, too, in relation to the speed of
travel. It is much easier to appreciate the essential completeness, the
unity in diversity of a place if you move through it slowly and care-

fully, physically feeling each slight change in terrain, every nuance
of difference. Walking on a road holds you away from this to some
degree, though nothing like driving does. I did hope to leave the
road wherever possible and see what walking through the untouched northern Yukon wilderness was like.

I was packing up when Dawna came over. "Come and say
good-bye," she said. I did, over my third breakfast or perhaps an
early lunch, this time soup, bread, and handfuls of dried fruit. The
meal over and their motorbikes laden, Dawna and Ian headed south.
I felt a sense of loss. Close communication with others is rare on a
long walk and disturbs the sense of self-contained isolation I usually feel in the wilderness. But of course I wasn't in the wilderness.
I was on the road.

Well, almost on the road. Lil Canyon, which runs parallel to
the highway, gave me four miles of solitude and a reprieve from
human artifacts before the road dominated the rest of the day. From
the pleasant rocky ravine I had my final views of the distant tiny
pyramid of Tombstone Mountain. I was saddened at turning away
from that wonderful land. It had been and would remain the high
point of the walk, the place where everything meshed together and I
was at one with myself and the wilderness.

Lil Creek was lined with the usual dense willows, beyond
which rose cliffs of loose rock, so for much of the way I walked in
the shallow water, staring down at the long swirling strands of
bright green weed wrapping themselves sensuously around shiny
stones. Dark clouds brought light rain and rumbles of thunder.

I came out on the highway a half mile or so south of North
Fork Pass, where I crossed the Continental Divide—another first for
the walk. The waters of the East Blackstone River, whose valley I
now followed, ended up in the Arctic rather than in the Pacific
Ocean. I was entering the main southern Ogilvie Mountains, a vast
range that sweeps across the northern Yukon in a great westward-
trending curve. They include the Tombstone Range, though these
granite mountains differ from the rest of the Ogilvies, which are

composed mostly of sedimentary rock. The terrain is all above timberline, here at three thousand feet. I left the last trees at Tombstone Recreational Park. Rugged peaks, their sides scooped out into great cirques, rise on either side of the highway. Unusually, and unlike the mountains to the north and the Klondike hills to the south, the southern Ogilvies were heavily glaciated during the Ice Age and characterize ice-carved mountains. That evening I found a fine campsite on a gravel bar beside the East Blackstone River. Plentiful driftwood made for a good fire.

The Dempster isn't a highway in the normal sense but simply a ninety-foot-wide strip of gravel stretching 460 miles from the Klondike Highway in the south to Inuvik on the Mackenzie Delta in the north. Apart from a few highway maintenance camps, a handful of basic campgrounds, the Eagle Plains Hotel at the halfway point, and the small native communities of Fort McPherson and Arctic Red River in the Northwest Territories, the route is lined by nothing but subarctic wilderness. Kilometer posts mark the distance traveled from the southern start of the highway. One problem for the walker is that you can't kid yourself you've walked farther than you have!

The road was built to exploit the oil reserves of the far north. Construction was begun in 1958 but halted in 1961 after seventy-two miles because exploration had not revealed much oil. The possibility of an oil pipeline running through the northern Yukon following the discovery of vast oil reserves at Prudhoe Bay in Alaska stimulated renewed work on the road a decade later, and it was finally finished in 1979. Oil has still not been found in large quantities, and the pipeline remains only a possibility. For the sake of the environment and the wildlife along the Dempster, it is hoped that it will remain so. As it is, the highway has affected the land on either side in a major way. Strict regulations had to be enacted to control hunting along the road and the use of off-road vehicles; within a few years of the highway opening, the once abundant moose had almost disappeared from the roadside forests. No hunting or firearms discharge is allowed for a half mile on either side of the highway between Kilometer 68 (Mile 42) and the border with the Northwest Territories, while off-road vehicles may not be used within five miles of the road. Campgrounds like the Tombstone Recreational Park have been built to limit the impact of visitors who wish to spend nights out in the wilderness.

Before the coming of the highway, the northern Yukon was little known except to the small number of natives of the Kutchin tribe, perhaps fifteen hundred in total, who lived there and an even smaller number of white trappers, hunters, and prospectors who occasionally ventured into it. The latter stuck to the rivers and valleys and made no attempt to explore the mountains until 1888 when William Ogilvie linked the Yukon and Peel river systems by an overland route.

The first European communities sprang up on the shores of the Arctic Ocean at Fort McPherson and Herschel Island for the purposes of fur trapping and whaling. Both soon had Mounted Police posts, set up in part to reinforce Canada's claim to the Arctic coast. In order to maintain contact between these far northern outposts and Dawson City, where there was a telegraph post, the police ran annual dogsled patrols from 1904 until 1921, when radio communications ended the need. Overland travel was easier in winter despite the extreme cold and severe storms because the obstructing swamps and rivers were frozen solid.

All the patrols, except one, started from the south because better supplies were available in Dawson. The 475-mile route, used for centuries by the Kutchin Indians, went through Seela Pass in the Cloudy Range, then down the west fork of the Blackstone River before crossing the line of the present highway at Kilometer 115 (Mile 71). It then continued via the Hart and Wind rivers to Fort McPherson.

In 1911 The Lost Patrol started from Fort McPherson. They made it to the Wind River but then went fatally astray, losing the route deep in the wilderness. The men tried to return to Fort

McPherson but died of exhaustion and starvation just twenty-five miles from their destination. It is a grim and chilling story and one that prefigured a similar event on the other side of the world a year later when Antarctic explorer Captain Robert Scott and his companions died close to a food cache in similar circumstances on their return from the South Pole.

When the patrol did not arrive in Dawson, a rescue team led by Corporal Jack Dempster was sent out. They traveled the trail in record time and quickly located the missing men, but too late. Their return to Dawson with the sad news took just nineteen days. One result of the tragedy was that, unlike The Lost Patrol, all subsequent patrols included a native guide. Food caches were set out too, and the trail blazed and marked. Dempster went on to become an inspector and to make more winter patrols between Dawson and Fort McPherson than anyone else and to hold speed records in both directions.

Early the next morning I passed by the RCMP (who still patrol the area, though now in well-equipped motor vehicles) as they attended to an upturned camper in the mud below the road. Soon afterward I came upon another vehicle parked by the roadside. The woman inside told me that her husband had just gone into the bush to photograph a caribou they had seen. "He'd love to do what you're doing," she said.

Dominating the view was the volcanolike cone of fifty-five-hundred-foot Mount Vines, also known as Pilot's Peak because it serves as a landmark for light aircraft that anglers, hunters, and out-fitters use to reach deep into the bush. The open landscape along the Blackstone River, where the mountains lie farther back from the road, made for good birdwatching possibilities. I saw several ptarmigan on the lower slopes of the mountains and many ravens soaring overhead. A peregrine falcon, fast and lethal, shot across the sky while two large birds of prey circled, too far away for clear identification.

All too soon I left the southern Ogilvies behind for the more gentle though still steep-sided, scree-covered, pale limestone hills of the northern Ogilvies. Light forest—spruce, willow, and aspen—began to appear, just in time to provide shelter from a heavy shower. For the first time on the walk I erected the tarp as a lunchtime shelter, pegging it out over a steep bank among willows right on the edge of the East Blackstone River, whose name comes from the seams of coal found in places in its banks.

The rain cleared. A lovely evening light made the mountains glow as I wandered down a side track back to the Blackstone looking for a place to camp. A big fire ring revealed a well-used off-road site on the bank. It was a beautiful spot, with the river on either side and beyond it a wide plain of bush and swamp stretching away to the distant mountains glowing golden in the evening sun. The vast sky dominated the land, and there was a great sense of space and openness, creating a feeling of freedom that I've experienced only in northern wildernesses. A fine sunset added to the pleasures of the site, as did being out of sight and almost out of sound of the road.

A further cause for joy was that, after a day and a half on the highway, I was heading up into the mountains, cutting a corner of the road with a climb up fifty-eight-hundred-foot Mount Distincta, one of the highest peaks in the northern Ogilvie range. The bare southeastern slopes of the mountains almost reach the road at one point, leaving little undergrowth to be tackled before the ascent began. Although there was no sign of a trail, the hiking was easy if steep in places, for the broad ridges consisted mainly of small, flat stones. As I climbed, wave after wave of long mountain ridges appeared, and it became apparent that the northern Ogilvies were made up of huge elongated piles of gray limestone rubble, banded in places with long thin lines of red and gold.

Mount Distincta, or Distincta Peak—depending on which map you consult—had a tall green plastic tower on its summit, a double of the one on top of Caribou Mountain. The views were extensive, revealing the almost unbelievable vastness of the northern Yukon wilderness. The mountains simply disappeared into the distant horizon in every direction.

A long, steep, and slippery descent down endless scree and talus slopes led to Windy Pass, a narrow, steep-sided cleft separating the Blackstone River and Engineer Creek, both of which drain into the Peel River. My hopes of camping high had been dashed by the total absence of water on the rocky ridges. Down in the valley I soon found a stream on the Engineer Creek side of the pass. Cold rain began to fall just after I lit a fire. I gulped down some food and headed for the shelter of the tent. Lying down earlier than expected was good for my feet. After fourteen miles of steep, rocky slopes they ached more than they had for weeks.

Little was left of the food supplies I had carried from Dawson, necessitating a brisk twenty-three-miles hike the next day to my next supply point at Mile 122. The walk down the narrow, V-shaped, densely wooded Engineer Creek valley was made memorable by the first fall colors, splashes of bright yellow with touches of deep red among the sober greens. They weren't enough to hold my attention for long, though, and I read *Nicholas Nickelby* much of the way. Road walking was becoming tedious. At least bushwhacking required concentration and effort. It might be frustrating and exhausting, but that was better than boring. At one point I noticed the creek was rust colored and the banks were stained brown and red. I learned later that iron oxide brought down by a side creek caused the discoloration and that the water is unsafe to drink. Big Creek was renamed Engineer Creek in 1971 to commemorate the engineers of the Department of Public Works who had worked on the Dempster Highway in this area.

"Come and have a coffee." Two trail-stained, sunburned figures were sitting under a dirty orange tarp just off the road. A big fire blazed in front of them, a pot of coffee situated somewhat precariously at its edge. A pair of worn leather saddles, a chain saw, and a green sleeping bag lay on the ground. Two horses grazed nearby. The couple were both dressed in check shirts, jeans, and heavy-duty hiking boots. The man also sported a leather cowboy hat and a thick black beard. His accent proclaimed him a French Canadian. The woman told me she was a local native Indian. They had just come out of the bush after four days in the Hart River area to the east where they had been prospecting for gold and other minerals. They worked under a government grant and had collected many rock samples. Their pack animals, a horse and a mule, had gone astray, they said, seemingly unconcerned. "Oh, it's happened before. They always turn up eventually." The previous night they'd had no rain and had slept out under a tree. I asked about the horses and they said traveling with them was difficult in the muskeg and it was often easier to lead the horses on foot. They didn't cover many miles each day.

We talked for half an hour or so, the conversation ranging widely, covering at one point the Salman Rushdie affair—"He's ahead of his time," was the man's opinion. "The Muslims aren't ready for criticism"—and at another the prospector's bad luck with cameras. He had fallen into a creek earlier in the year and ruined one camera, so he bought a waterproof one that he'd lost two days into this trip.

Engineer Creek Recreational Park was situated among tall willows and a few spruce and aspen under the impressive castellated limestone ridge of Sapper Hill. Like the creek, the hill was named in 1971 to commemorate work on the highway, in this case by the Royal Canadian Engineers (known like army engineers for centuries as sappers) who had built the bridge over the Ogilvie River here.

I arrived at the campground after ten and a half hours and the highest one-day mileage so far. Early the next morning rain had me erecting the tarp over a picnic table, with my staff and tripod called into service as makeshift poles. There were lots of bugs about, mostly blackflies and only a few mosquitoes, but a smoldering mosquito coil under the tarp repelled them. The woman in the nature interpretative center at the Tombstone campground had warned me about this problem. "Built on a swamp," she explained.

I had no food left at all, so breakfast was just a cup of coffee. I had had stewed figs for the last two mornings. My supplies lay only a step away, however, at the highway maintenance camp just across the Ogilvie River. The people there were friendly and curious to meet this wanderer whose food they had been storing for the last two weeks. "You must be getting sick of dried food," they said, adding a bag of freshly baked pastries and apples to my two food boxes.

Back at the campground I unpacked the supply boxes onto the picnic table, curious to find out exactly what I had. Coffee, sugar, two packets of granola, a bag of trail mix, ten packets of soup, ten freeze-dried entrées, twenty vitamin-C drink packets, eighteen Bear Valley MealPack bars, twenty granola bars, three boxes of matches (which I didn't need), a spare headlamp battery (which I did; I'd been using my lamp more than expected on several late nights), maps, and a paperback book spilled out. All that was lacking was dried milk. It seemed an awful lot, but I knew it would disappear fast, and it was far less than I'd had when I left Dawson. My plans were to reach Eagle Plains in ten days. Looking at my supplies I decided that if I didn't want to be hungry I needed to cut that to eight. Reading about the Lost Patrol didn't encourage me to take too many risks without supplies!

Out of idle curiosity I worked out from the details on the wrappers that my basic diet provided only 2,837 calories. For the last three days it had been less than two thousand per day. On long walks I normally need at least four thousand calories a day. This explained why I had lost weight since Dawson and had to use a piece of cord to hold up my pants. On most days I had eaten more than the basic, as I usually stocked up on cheese, biscuits, and dried fruit wherever there was a store. I had also been mostly ahead of schedule and so had extra dried food. But along the Dempster Highway, Eagle Plains was the only place with a store. Most people I met offered me food, but I hardly wanted to rely on handouts.

I spent the rest of the day under the tarp mulling over the maps. Outside, the rain poured steadily. I had planned a day off here anyway. What I hadn't planned was my route for the next few days. I did not want to walk the 110 miles to Eagle Plains on the road. There seemed to be two other options: a high route to the east, a valley route to the west. Both would probably be difficult, but only the first involved crossing any major rivers. I postponed making a decision until the next morning.

There were few other people around. A couple standing by the roadside were trying to hitch a lift south in order to get a spare tire for their car, since the maintenance camp did not have the right size. They had bumped slowly past me the previous afternoon, their burst tire a mass of shredded rubber. I was amazed that anyone would travel a remote highway without carrying a spare. Personally I'd take two.

During the evening, Greg, a tall, lean, fair-haired man who worked at the maintenance camp, turned up with a bottle of Wiser's Deluxe Canadian Whisky. We spent an entertaining hour and a half drinking it. A few mud-spattered vehicles rolled in to the campground. After Greg had departed for home, one of the new arrivals, a heavily built, sparkling-eyed Indian from Pelly Crossing named Alec Isaac, came over with a jug of California Chablis of which he drank a fair amount and I, already a little fuzzy from the whiskey, just a little. He was here to hunt moose, he said, but made it clear that he never ventured far from the road. The next morning he and his wife, who remembered the piece in the *Yukon News*—now two months old—stopped by to say farewell and to take my picture.

Before I left, Greg reappeared. It was still raining. Between eight the night before and eight that morning the maintenance camp weather station had recorded more than half an inch of rain. Engineer Creek and the Ogilvie River were both noticeably higher than on the day before, and the soft, muddy highway quickly clogged my boots. The mountaintops were shrouded in cloud.

The high route seemed inadvisable, especially as river crossings were involved, so I went west along the banks of the surging Ogilvie River. The initial going along shingle banks and through fairly open spruce forest over surprisingly firm ground was quite good, but even so I felt a strong urge to return to the highway and take the easy route to Eagle Plains. I resisted, knowing I would soon feel at home again in the wilderness. After a couple of hours I came to steep black shale bluffs split by a recent landslide that I had to climb up and around. If I had met this obstacle nearer the road I might have turned back.

A large patch of willow-dotted gravel and mud (sand when dry, I guessed) jutting out into the river made a good campsite. I lit a driftwood fire in front of the tarp to stave off the cold and wet. Out to the west a thin line of bright sky was visible and an occasional gust of wind blew, harbingers, I hoped, of better weather. This was the first camp since Divide Lake, a week earlier, that hadn't been beside the highway. Maybe that was why I was showing signs of dependence on that thin gravel line. I had to keep off the road in my head as well as with my feet.

Settling down in front of the fire, I began to read the paperback book from my Engineer Creek cache, Anthony Burgess's *Any Old Iron,* and was immediately amazed at how some of the Welsh characters attacked Saxons in just the same way fire ranger Bill Jackson had lectured me. He could have read the book, of course, but I doubted it.

Though the night had been dry I woke the next morning to find myself on an island. The river had risen several feet, and the old silted-up channel—the remains of an oxbow lake—that lay between my camp and the main bank was now swirling with water. I rushed out of the tent to check on my food bags, which I had left only thirty feet or so from the water's edge. They were still there, but the river was just ten feet away. I stuck a stick in the water. An hour later it showed that the river had risen another few inches.

Since my boots were already wet, I kept them on for the knee-deep ford back to the bank. Progress that morning was slow, the terrain along the river consisting of bogs, wet brush, swollen side creeks, backwaters, dense timber, slippery rocks, steep cliffs, and rock slides. A long, boggy, flat area looked as though it might be the backcountry airstrip marked on the map that I hoped might have a trail leading north.

And it did, a reasonable trail that led through a narrow gap in the hillside to a vast wide-open muskeg area dotted with an occasional stand of black spruce, through which wound two creeks. According to the map my route lay between them. Isolated limestone hills broke the skyline on either side.

I had not ventured far into this broad valley when I spotted a black object a quarter of a mile away to the west that looked suspiciously like a large animal. Through my binoculars I saw a dark grizzly bear foraging, I guessed, for berries. Although it was farther away than the one I saw from the Tombstone campground, because I was alone in the wilderness this bear was more awe inspiring and more frightening. I felt privileged to see it, as only a few hundred grizzlies inhabit the whole of the Ogilvies. Compared with the better-known coastal bears of Alaska and British Columbia, the northern Yukon grizzlies are small, the males reaching no more than five hundred pounds, females two-thirds of that, because of the sparse food available. Knowing these details didn't detract from the impressiveness of this bear. Meeting the unchallenged lord of the mountains, the ultimate symbol of wilderness, can never be less than exhilarating.

I passed by the bear on the east side of the valley, watching it from time to time. I don't think it ever knew I was there. The blackflies did. Hordes of them. A good coating of repellent on my skin stopped them from biting but not from flying constantly into my face. For the first time I wore the repellent-impregnated mesh head net I was carrying, draping it over my Tilley hat, then tightening it around my throat. It was very stuffy inside, but the net kept the flies out.

Skirting the bear pushed me farther east than I had intended and away from the westernmost of the creeks, beside which I could see potential campsites. I wasn't going to challenge the grizzly's rights to that valley, though. The other creek produced just tussocks, wet holes and slopes, and a scattering of black spruce. "There is always somewhere to camp," I told myself, then set out determinedly to find it. I finally set up my kitchen just above the creek on sloping ground, choosing the spot because there was a patch of bare earth nearby where I could light a fire without leaving a scar, and several fallen dead spruce lay not far away for firewood. Despite my digging out a pit, even the fire was on a slope. And so was the tent, higher up the hillside. I padded the underside of my sleeping mat with clothes, trying to produce a reasonably level bed.

No wilderness camp is ever totally forgettable, and that evening as I was eating dinner a light shower fell, followed immediately by a full rainbow shining across the hills to the east. After the shower the air felt fresh and clear and the flies vanished. The temperature was just thirty-seven degrees Fahrenheit, but it felt warmer than it had for days because the air was drier. The sky cleared and a few stars appeared. Then, tantalizingly, for just a few minutes a flicker of pale green stretched across the sky. Despite the first below-freezing temperature of the walk (thirty degrees) and the sloping site, I slept well. Ice coated the edge of the fly sheet at dawn.

Three more exhausting days of slow progress and difficult walking through muskeg and black spruce forest followed. Blackflies plagued me much of the time, and I made many cold, knee-deep creek fords. There were also rewards, both spiritual and physical. Below the limestone-tower-topped bare screes of Transplant Mountain I walked through a magnificent grove of majestic balsam poplars and white spruce, the biggest trees I had seen on the walk. Beyond them I came upon a cut line, a leftover from the days of oil exploration, with a good trail running down the middle. This led to another crossing of the Continental Divide, here a wide, gentle pass between the drainages of the Ogilvie and Whitestone rivers.

Ahead lay open country and more cross-country travel through bogs and tussocks and deep, soft moss. A pale-headed owl slipped silently out of the grasses just in front of me, and I saw several piles of freshly churned earth where grizzlies had been digging for ground squirrels. Gnawed moose antlers, pale and flat, lay on the ground.

On my fourth night away from the highway I camped on the edge of the forest between scattered small black spruce and thicker groves of white spruce. A thin streak of northern lights cut across the sky, then faded and died. I left the tent door open in case they recurred. At midnight they did, and I was quickly outside, watching great waves of green surge out of the northern horizon and sweep the sky. The solid sheets meshed, twisted into themselves, and became huge pulsing spirals of eerie light snaking across the sky from horizon to horizon. I lay on my back, oblivious to the frozen ground, entranced by the unearthly glory of this spectacular display. Only the silhouettes of a few tall spruce against the sky reminded me I was still on this planet. After an hour the lights began to fade. The show was over. Stiff with cold, I slid into the sleeping bag.

After crossing the Divide again I followed a tributary of the Ogilvie River east, making one last camp three miles before rejoining the highway. It was so calm I could hear the occasional vehicle. An animal moving outside the tent woke me before dawn, but I saw nothing except an ominous red slash across the eastern horizon. Gear I'd left under the tarp had been pushed about but not damaged. Porcupine? I wondered.

Bright orange flagging led to a barely perceptible horse trail that I followed to where it burst abruptly through bushes onto the highway near Kilometer 236 (Mile 146.5). I had been in the backcountry for just over four days yet had walked barely forty-six miles. I was also only twenty-six miles from where I had left the Dempster, no more than a day's walk on the road. Eagle Plains still lay eighty miles away. I didn't regret my loop into the wilderness. It had been hard and at times frustrating, but it had also been fulfilling in a way that walking up a road could never be. All day every day I had been absorbed in the minutiae of wilderness walking, constantly looking at where I put my feet, always thinking of the route, scanning the land for bears, considering where to ford creeks and whether to go over or around ridges and hills. This was total travel requiring total involvement. Walking the Dempster merely meant keeping going.

Even on the highway there was still the pattern of clouds in the sky and the shapes of the mountains and the colors of the vegetation. Next to the highway, ran the Ogilvie River, a fine, wide river with many islets and sandbars and rushing channels. The willows and tamaracks lining the banks were turning yellow, gold, and red, and the view east to the now distant mountains was beautiful. I detoured down a side track for fifty yards to lunch by the river and, as it was sunny, spread out my gear, wet from the days of rain and slogging through swamps.

As I sat on the bank gazing at the swirling water, I sensed something moving behind me. Very slowly and quietly I turned around. A large gray wolf and a smaller black one were scavenging among garbage that had been left by horse parties who had used the track as a campsite. My camera was lying next to me, fortunately already out of its noisy, Velcro-fastened case, and I managed to take a couple of shots before the animals noticed me and slipped quickly but silently into the bushes.

Shortly after I rejoined it the Dempster Highway left the Ogilvie River and started the climb to the area known, inaccurately, as Eagle Plains. The name is ill-fitting not only because this region is one of rolling hills rather than plains, but also because it's the one area of the Yukon where eagles are least likely to be seen. The name actually comes from the Eagle River, which forms the northern boundary of the "plain" and has its source in the area.

The highway mostly follows the height of the land across Eagle Plains, often running along the Continental Divide, and so is the best route for walkers as well as drivers. As Eagle Plains is mostly covered with dense stunted black spruce forest and muskeg, off-road travel would not have been as pleasant, easy, or scenic. Dwindling supplies meant I needed to reach Eagle Plains Lodge as quickly as possible anyway.

There was one potential problem with walking the road. "Water is almost totally unavailable in this region," wrote Walter Lanz in *Along the Dempster,* his guide to the road and its environs. I only needed tiny seeps, however, for my needs and I had found these in other apparently waterless areas, so I expected I could there, too, especially with so much wet boggy ground. Even so, I left the Ogilvie River with both quart water bottles full.

Ironically, I passed several tiny creeks during the steep thousand-foot climb out of the Ogilvie River valley. The long winding ascent gave superb views of the long, distant line of the Ogilvie Mountains shining in the evening light beyond the sparkling sinuous ribbon of river. As I approached the crest of the hills a large, white, block-shaped structure appeared off to the side of the road some distance ahead. Curious, and hopeful it might be an open cabin, I investigated. A truck-size vehicle shed made of timber panels stood at the end of a wide gravel cutting. A small side door was unlocked. Inside I found the shed was just a shell with an earthen floor. It would do for a night, and I set up camp in a corner, using the tarp as a groundsheet, then went in search of water. A hundred yards away I found a puddle in the muskeg. It was enough.

The next day saw me heading straight into the worst storm of the trip. Head down I struggled into the strong, cold northeast wind and the lashing torrential rain. There was little shelter, as I was on the highest section of the road where it crosses large areas of open alpine tundra. At a rest area people in a pickup with canoes on the roof told me it was snowing farther north.

Coming upon a black spruce thicket in a dip, I slung the tarp between the trees and huddled under it while I heated up soup for a warming lunch. It was fifty-two degrees but felt far colder. I considered my position. I had little food left, and my next supplies were at least three days away. I was on a road and not in the backcountry, however, so there was an alternative. I took it, deciding to hitchhike to Eagle Plains, then return to my pickup point and continue the walk. Slogging along wet and miserable in a storm on short rations when it wasn't necessary seemed pointless. Although this was in a sense breaking the continuity of the walk, I soon rationalized it away. Going on ahead for supplies didn't compromise my one rule for long walks, which is to walk every step of the way, except where unfordable rivers or lakes have to be crossed.

Within minutes of my packing up the tarp, a van, the first vehicle to pass, stopped, convincing me my decision was the right one. It was packed with photographers on a tour out of Vancouver, photographing the fall colors. They were heading for Eagle Plains and managed to squeeze me in among the camera bags and heavy-duty tripods. The talk was, unsurprisingly, of photography, and they were astonished at how little equipment I had. I assured them that if they were on foot and had to carry it all on their backs, it would soon seem too much.

Soon I was sloshing through the mud to the motel–highway maintenance camp complex of Eagle Plains. The wet and windswept campground there wasn't conducive to relaxed camping, so I checked into a room for two nights. It was twenty days since I had left Dawson, and although I'd had two rest days on campgrounds, I needed to sort out gear, write letters and notes, wash clothes and—for other people's sake as well as my own—take a shower. I relished the thought of real meals in a restaurant, too. The small store had limited backpacking supplies—ramen noodles, candy, and Kool-Aid—and I was glad I hadn't planned on stocking up here. Behind the counter they had a welcome bundle of letters for me. The food supplies were at the gas station.

Chores done, I spent my rest day writing letters over several meals and much coffee. This was probably my last chance to send mail before the walk was over. There was only one collection a week, but one of the photographers, Graeme McCahon, lately from

British Columbia and originally from Australia, kindly offered to post my mail, which included twenty-five rolls of film. I also arranged to leave most of my food plus surplus gear in the hotel for my return in a couple of days.

Getting back to where the photographers had picked me up proved difficult. After a morning spent waiting in vain for traffic to pass, I returned to the hotel for lunch. A sunburned man with a long pony tail, a fleece jacket, denim jeans, and a battered North Face pack gravitated toward me, recognizing, I think, a fellow wilderness wanderer. His name was Paul Morley and he had just finished a 750-mile canoe journey with three others down the Bell, Porcupine, and Yukon rivers to Fairbanks, Alaska. He had hitchhiked back to pick up his van, only to find that it was in Dawson. He had told the hotel manager to let anyone drive it there who would fill it with gas. Someone had. Now he had to hitchhike back down the highway. "Wish I'd called to check," he said.

We sat outside atop a gravel heap on a caribou hide Paul pulled from his pack, watching the empty road. "Winter is the time to be up here," Paul told me, "because you can travel easily on the snow and river ice." That's what the natives traditionally do, he went on, summer being for chores. Paul always canoed, telling me he carried too much photographic gear to backpack anyway, though he was not averse to portaging equipment and canoes over high mountain passes between river systems when necessary. He had explored much of the northern Yukon and Alaska and had paddled in the Arctic Ocean. By comparison mine was just a fleeting visit that barely touched the area. I had already decided I wanted to come back, perhaps for a winter ski trip.

It was well into the afternoon before one of the few vehicles on the road stopped, a heavily laden pickup with room for only one. The couple inside were heading for Dawson, but slowly, taking four days for the journey. As it would take me my fifty miles in one go, the ride went to me, Paul hastily scribbling his addresses in Fairbanks and Seattle on a book of matches as I left. (He told me in a note a few months later that he got a ride to Dawson soon afterward.)

The young couple in the pickup were from Vancouver and on their honeymoon, which they were spending on a camping, fishing, and hunting trip through British Columbia and the Yukon. "You're the Englishman we've heard about," said the woman after I outlined the story of the walk. The evening after I left the Engineer Campground, they had been there and met Alec Isaac, who mentioned me.

At 4:15 P.M. we reached the area where I thought the photographers had stopped for me. My bootprints were still clearly visible, caked into the now dry mud. I had remembered the spot well: just seven minutes after I started walking again I came upon the exact spot where I had been picked up, the tire marks of the van as it pulled off the road and my footprints walking over to it telling the story.

The fall colors were at their height, an impressionistic wash of brilliant reds and yellows against a canvas of green and gray. Far ahead I could see the tiny outline of the Richardson Mountains and, slightly closer, a silvery smudge on a hilltop that had to be the Eagle Plains buildings. Twice I found the tracks of a small bear on the roadside, and once a red fox trotted across the gravel in front of me.

The late start meant I began looking for a campsite after only twelve miles. A gravel pit containing a few shallow pools of water looked a possibility until I noticed a small building at the far end of it, an unlocked cabin made from wood paneling clearly used by trappers in the winter. There was a distressing amount of junk strewn all around outside, but inside it was clean and there were tables and chairs and a bunk bed. No one would mind or even know if I stayed the night, so I moved in.

Two more days on the road and I was back at the Eagle Plains Hotel. The hiking was uneventful, the fall colors being the main attraction. For several hours I walked through the area that had been burned in the big fire that I'd heard about at Fort Selkirk. The road had been closed for several days while the forest burned. It was easy to see why. Black skeletal trees, their charred bark hanging from them, lined the highway, the ground under them dark with charcoal and dust. Nothing grew or moved and there was no color. Occasionally swathes of green cut through the grim ghost forest, startlingly bright and fresh and alive.

"Want a ride?" "No thanks, I'm walking." My reply was automatic. There were a few such offers each day. One driver couldn't believe my reply. "What, for the exercise?" he joked. When I refused a lift a second time he looked worried. "You're sure you're all right?" he muttered, clearly convinced I wasn't. The photographers passed, heading back south, and stopped to tell me they had been up the highway to the Richardson Mountains and it was snowing there. They loaded me up with apples, oranges, cheese, rye bread, and salami before they departed.

Farther on, the water truck from Eagle Plains stopped. All the water for the hotel and highway camp is brought up from nearby rivers and creeks, work that has to be done every day, so these trucks go constantly up and down the highway. The truck driver told me two small grizzlies had been seen near the hotel the previous night, a piece of information that settled the debate I was having with myself whether to camp or check into a room. For peace of mind it would be the room.

That evening in the hotel I was told that grizzlies often wandered around outside but never bothered anybody. Compared with the near paranoia I had encountered farther south, the view here seemed almost blasé.

Before I left Eagle Plains I phoned Peter Novak of CBC radio in Whitehorse, as I had arranged to do at the start of the walk. He told me they had already had snow. As he interviewed me about the walk, I began to realize it was nearly over, that within two weeks I would heft my pack for the last time and my life would change. It was not a happy thought. I didn't want to stop.

9

Into the Arctic:
The Richardson
Mountains

EAGLE PLAINS TO THE DEMPSTER
HIGHWAY

AUGUST 31–SEPTEMBER 8, 80 MILES

Driving snow, a wind that cut like a
white-hot knife, and darkness, had
forced them to grope for a camping
place.

—Jack London, *The Call of
the Wild*

Despite leaving a bag of used maps and books, spare clothes, the fire grill, and other odds and ends at Eagle Plains, to be picked up on my journey south after the walk was over, I set off for the Richardson Mountains with the heaviest load of the walk. As I didn't know what to expect in this last mountain section of the trek, I was carrying dehydrated food for two weeks, augmented with chocolate bars, one and a half pounds of cheese, a pound of Dutch chocolate instant coffee—a curious concoction that was the only coffee the hotel store had—plus several packets of Kool-Aid.

My plan was to follow the highway the twenty-seven miles to the edge of the mountains, then make my way north along the crest of the Richardsons. When I reached the highway again where it turned east and crossed the mountains, leaving the Yukon, I would decide whether to go on or finish there.

I had previously worn my better-cushioned running shoes for road walking, but since I couldn't fit my boots in the bulging pack, I had to wear them. Luckily the day was ideal for comfortable walking—cool and breezy with some sun.

From Eagle Plains the highway descends to cross the Eagle River just downstream of where an extraordinary forty-eight-day manhunt by police in the winter of 1932 ended with the shooting dead of the man known as the Mad Trapper of Rat River. Leaning over the bridge looking at the placid stream winding through a fringe of willows and balsam poplars, I found it hard to imagine it as the scene of such a drama.

The events started when police visited a reclusive trapper known in Fort McPherson as Albert Johnson. Johnson lived in a tiny, remote cabin on the Rat River on the eastern edge of the Richardsons. The police were investigating a complaint that Johnson had been tampering with other people's traps, a minor and not uncommon offense. Johnson refused to allow the police in or even to speak to them. When they returned with a warrant, he opened fire, seriously wounding one constable. To save the life of their injured friend, the others retreated and undertook a desperate twenty-hour dogsled journey to the small settlement of Aklavik.

The police returned in force, and Johnson was eventually forced out of his cabin after a siege that ended when the police blew off the roof with dynamite. The hunt was on, but another thirty-three days passed before police cornered Johnson and shot him out on the ice of Eagle River. During most of the chase he eluded his pursuers with ease, even though he was on snowshoes and carrying a heavy pack, while they were traveling by dogsled. He also engaged them in several more gunfights, during which he killed one constable before escaping up an ice cliff. Then, in a blizzard that brought the pursuit to a standstill, Johnson crossed the Richardson Mountains, something the local natives said couldn't be done in winter. Throughout the hunt the temperature was never warmer than thirty below zero, and at times it dropped to fifty below. Whatever else he might have been, Johnson was clearly a superb backwoodsman and wilderness survival expert.

The hunt was broadcast on the radio, then just a novelty, and the public went out and bought wireless sets in huge numbers in order to follow the story. The RCMP, for the first time, used an airplane, flown with great skill by "Wop" May, one of the first bush pilots. The plane proved to be the decisive factor in bringing the chase to an end. As well as providing aerial scouting, it was invaluable in bringing in supplies for the pursuers, cutting down the resupply time from three days to less than half an hour.

Who the fugitive was has never been conclusively established, though Dick North makes a good case in his excellent book *The Mad Trapper of Rat River* for his being an itinerant woodsman of Swedish origin named Arthur Nelson. No one knows why he first shot at the police. Was he the perpetrator of a ghastly crime or simply a loner suffering from "cabin fever" who had cracked under the strain? Whatever the facts, his story is now part of the North.

Beyond the river the road climbs continuously for five miles to the foothills of the Richardsons, an ascent I found tiring despite the distractions of the beautiful fall colors and the views of the mountains. The Gold City Tours minibus, heading south, stopped, giving me the opportunity to thank the driver for delivering my food boxes. I camped next to the road above the trees on a brilliant red and yellow carpet of alpine vegetation. Cars swept past, their headlights momentarily lighting up the camp. I wondered what their occupants made of the flicker of the fire and the glow of my headlamp.

Heavy rain fell all night and into the morning. Low clouds brushed the tops of the trees and hid the hills from view. The temperature was a miserable thirty-seven degrees. It was just ten miles to the foot of Mount Hare, where I intended to camp the next night, so an early start wasn't necessary. I snuggled down into my warm sleeping bag.

The skies began to clear early in the afternoon and the mountains, lightly covered with fresh snow, appeared under patches of blue sky. I set off, but the storm had only paused for breath, and a cold northwest wind soon brought in more rain and sleet. I stomped on, wondering if I were going to get off the highway at all. I didn't want to finish the walk like this.

A distraction was provided at Kilometer 403 (Mile 250), as here the Dempster Highway crosses the Arctic Circle, that imaginary line at 66°33´ north which is the southernmost edge of the area where the sun remains above the horizon for twenty-four hours on the summer solstice. Even though I was on a road, and even though I knew the Circle was a human creation, I still felt excited. I was entering the Arctic, that romantic, dangerous, exciting world that had enthralled me since I was a child. The word stands in my mind as a symbol of pure wilderness, of unsullied beauty. I had in fact crossed the Arctic Circle once before, in Finnish Lapland, but in a vehicle rather than on foot, a method of travel I felt didn't count as a true journey. Now for the first time I was entering the Arctic on foot and about to explore a range of mountains about which I knew little. Arctic explorer Sir John Franklin, the first European to enter the Yukon and whose later disappearance in the Arctic Ocean had been one of the great mysteries of the Arctic, named the mountains for Sir John Richardson. Richardson was the surgeon and naturalist on Franklin's land-based expeditions in search of the Northwest Passage in 1819–20 and 1825–27. I found this faint link with the past quite thrilling.

Roald Amundsen was another great polar explorer who traveled through the northern Yukon. Amundsen is most famous for being the first man to reach the South Pole, but he also completed the first successful navigation of the Northwest Passage. Having reached the whaling station at Herschel Island in the fall of 1905, where his ship *Gjöa* froze in along with many other ships, Amundsen wanted to let the world know of his success as quickly as possible. The nearest telegraph station was five hundred miles away at Eagle City on the Yukon River in Alaska. Amundsen set off for there with two Inuit, who were carrying mail from the whaling fleet, and William Mogg, the sixty-year-old captain of a wrecked whaler who was making for San Francisco in search of another ship. Although it was October, still early in the winter season, they traveled with two sledges and twelve dogs. Only Captain Mogg rode on a sledge, the Inuit using snowshoes and Amundsen skis. Mogg financed the trek. Amundsen, totally penniless despite his triumph, was basically his guest. The difficult journey took forty-three days. They crossed the mountains to the Porcupine River and followed it southwest out of the Yukon and into Alaska before turning southeast up the Yukon River to reach Eagle City on December 5 in temperatures of minus sixty degrees Fahrenheit. The following March, Amundsen was back at Herschel Island to rejoin the *Gjöa* for the final leg to the Bering Sea. It would be thirty-four years before anyone repeated the journey.

The Arctic Circle is now a tourist attraction marked by a car park and a large sign and information display. When I arrived, one other person was there, a young Japanese who offered me coffee he had brewed on a stove set up in the back of his station wagon, which was crammed with camping gear. "I'm from Tokyo," he told me casually, "and on a tour of the world." He had started in June 1990 and would finish sometime in 1992. His English was minimal (and my Japanese nonexistent), but I gathered that after driving around North America he was going to motorbike across Australia and then hitchhike through Asia and Europe. It somehow seemed appropriate that I should meet at the Arctic Circle someone undertaking such an adventure. It isn't a place for the mundane. The coffee wasn't ordinary either. It was vile. Possibly the worst I've ever tasted.

I waved good-bye as the traveler headed off for Inuvik at the northern end of the Dempster. His schedule was hectic; he intended to be back in Dawson the next day. It was not a way I would have wanted to see the world. My own way didn't seem so attractive, however, as I plodded grimly up the highway in the continuing storm.

An untidy sprawl of small trees beside a creek below Mount Hare harbored an old packhorse camp that was flat and dry, and I camped there. The weather was suitable for my first-ever night out in the Arctic, with light snow falling and a temperature of just thirty-four degrees. I slung the tarp between poles left by the horse party, then lit a fire. Piles of logs lying around, plus the remnants of bough beds left by the previous campers—who did not practice minimum-impact camping—provided plentiful fuel. They had at least removed or burned their garbage.

The day dawned with the almost oppressive and suffocating silence that comes with snow. An inch or more had fallen overnight and a little was still coming down. I lit a fire again under the crisp, frosted tarp. There was ice on the water in my pans. I seemed to have arrived in the Arctic just as winter did.

Above me rose 4,073-foot Mount Hare, the second-highest peak in the southern Richardson Mountains and the start of my traverse of that range. The steep 2,100-foot ascent took three hours. The weather gradually improved and the peaks drifted out of the mist as I climbed, although far to the south dark clouds marked where the storm was still raging. The alpine tundra and loose, flat rocks on the bare mountains made for easy walking. The snow, no more than a few inches deep, was no hindrance. The hills were rounded, with steep sides cut by deep, V-shaped creek valleys. Like most of the Yukon's mountain ranges, the sedimentary Richardsons were never glaciated. The absence of cliffs, hanging valleys, and other glacial features makes them ideal mountains for the walker rather than the climber. Strong winds are common, however—a serious hazard in such a remote range, as I would discover.

From Mount Hare I followed the watershed four miles or so before dropping down from a low saddle to a small creek where I camped among the first willows I reached as I descended, a comfortable scenic site. I was content—and impressed. The Richardsons looked as though they would offer the finest walking and camping terrain of the whole walk and would make for a splendid finale. I just hoped I would be granted a few days of sunshine. The dull evening faded into a glowering darkness that seemed to typify the coming Arctic winter. Under the tarp, pitched against a steep bank, the faint heat of a small fire of dead willow sticks was surprisingly effective as I found when I ventured beyond it. It was wonderful to camp away from the Dempster. Of the past eight nights, five had been by the road, three in the Eagle Plains hotel.

A dense mist surrounded the tent when I woke. The temperature was twenty-four degrees, the coldest night yet, and my boots were frozen. I had to thaw them a little over the fire before I could force my feet into them. The mist, a sign that the weather had changed, soon retreated down the valley, to leave a blue sky and sunshine creeping down the hillside.

A glorious day, a truly magnificent mountain day ensued. I was ecstatic and in love with the wilderness. For twelve miles I drifted along the broad undulating crest of the Richardson Mountains. A cold wind kept the air clear, the distant views razor sharp. Around noon, high cirrus drifted in from the west. Soon afterward the southern sky was a sheet of stratus. The north, though, remained clear. I crossed the tracks of a fox and then those of a snowshoe hare in the thin snow. A golden eagle soared high above. A long, steep-sided, almost level ridge lay ahead, terminating at its west end at the peak of Chii Nabil Mountain.

I made camp due west of Chii Nabil by a tributary of the Rock River. Again I was in the shelter of some willows, though here there were also small spruce and a few birch trees. I was a few hundred feet above timberline at twenty-seven hundred feet. It was a perfect wilderness camp despite the cold, which froze the damp tent as soon as I took it out of its stuff sack. The only sound was the trickle of the creek. One of the joys of being away from the highway was the silence. Another was the solitude. Since seeing a small cairn on Mount Hare, I had seen no sign of people at all. Even the sky was clean, with not a vapor trail in sight. The pristine mountains made me feel privileged to be here and that my responsibilities were great. I was even more careful than usual to ensure I left no sign of my passing.

In the morning the red and yellow hillside blazed with light, the stunning colors unbelievably rich and deep. At twenty-one degrees, the temperature was the lowest of the walk. Another glorious day followed, though at a slightly lower elevation, as I cut around the edge of the Chii Nabil massif over undulating spurs and shallow creek valleys to a saddle above the headwaters of the Cornwall River. I wanted to follow the river to the base of a long, high ridge that led to Richardson Pass and the point where the Yukon Territory and Northwest Territories meet on the Dempster Highway. Sunshine, blue skies, spectacular scenery, beautiful colors, easy cross-country walking: it was a backpacker's paradise.

As the creek grew in size, shaley bluffs and small cliffs appeared on either side, and the willows and spruce became thicker and harder to force a way through. I walked on shingle banks beside the water, fording the creek many times. Thin cloud covered the sun enough to cut out any warmth, and my wet feet were soon cold. When a good site appeared a couple of miles sooner than I had planned to stop, I took it. A big log made a good backrest for my kitchen, which was situated on a shingle island between two branches of the creek—and there was plenty of driftwood for a big, warming fire. The steep-sided valley was beautiful, with many large white spruce and balsam poplars as well as clumps of dense willows. To the north I could see the long, almost level thirty-five-hundred-foot ridge that stretched nearly ten miles to Richardson Mountain Pass. The climb onto it appeared steep, while escaping down the sides looked very difficult, if even possible. Once on it I would probably be committed to walking the whole length. I was concerned about the high cirrus clouds, which spoke of an approaching storm, as the ridge didn't look the place to be in bad weather. But there was no real alternative.

I was right to be worried. A gusty southwest wind bringing heavy rain woke me during the night. At dawn the mountains were hidden in swirling cloud. The rain beat down, bouncing off the gravel. As a rest day, the first in eight days, seemed the only (and not unwelcome) choice, I pitched the tarp in the forest and moved my kitchen under it. By pegging the tarp close to the ground and keeping the profile low, I was able to keep out all the wind and rain. Indeed, it was drier under the tarp than in the tent, where the lack of ventilation caused condensation. The rain came in short heavy bursts, turning to hail at times. The temperature remained at forty-two degrees all day. Black clouds poured across the sky from the west. A touch of sunshine and glimpses of blue sky gave hopes of a clearance, but they were never more than momentary.

I idled away the time, making various plans for the next few days. If possible I wanted to do a loop north of the Dempster before finishing, though I knew the weather might prevent this. Walking the highway to Fort McPherson was another option. On a trip over to the tent, which involved fording a branch of the creek, I was surprised and a little alarmed to find a large pile of bear dung only ten feet from the door. I was sure it hadn't been there a few hours earlier.

A few mosquitoes came out in the evening as the skies finally cleared. I was glad to see the storm hadn't dumped any snow on the ridge. In fact, it seemed to have washed away what was there. The wind gained in strength though, roaring in the trees above the valley and shaking the tent. I went outside during the night to tighten the guylines and check that the stakes were secure.

Though clouds were still streaming across the sky, I moved on the next day, a difficult bushwhack leading down the valley to the base of the ridge. The direct ascent, above a small creek, was steep but easy and sheltered. The wind bit as soon as I reached the exposed ridgetop, a cold powerful gusting blast taking my breath away. This end of the ridge was broad and covered with soft alpine vegetation. I staggered along toward the first of a number of minor summits. After this there was a narrower section of rotten stubby pinnacles and heaps of large boulders covered with greasy moss. Everything was very loose. This nasty stuff slowed me down and I slithered and skidded about, clinging onto rocks and clambering over boulders. Whenever I could, I used the larger rocks to break the wind. The view was extensive, with mountains to the north, south, and east and rolling tundra to the west, and cutting across the tundra the dark line of the Dempster, not far away but a long way down.

Beyond the pinnacles the ridge climbed a little to another summit, which I tried to skirt on a shelf of boulders to the east. The wind heightened and blew me off my feet. I could now only progress by leaning so far sideways that I could use my hands to hold onto the rocks, almost crawling. I paused in the shelter of a boulder. What was I doing? This was both ridiculous and dangerous, the chance of breaking a limb high. I decided to abandon the ridge if I could. Knowing that forcing a way west to the highway would probably be impossible because of the wind, I gingerly descended the steep eastern slope, which was a mass of loose, slippery moss and boulders. There were no cliffs, so the going was rough but not really dangerous. My staff was essential. Without it I would have found keeping my balance difficult, especially given the weight and size of my pack.

Once onto easier ground at around twenty-three hundred feet, I headed north along the base of the ridge. To the east stretched a wide bare valley of mossy tussocks, stunted willow and birch, and small lakes that drained to the east by the Vittrekwa River. It was a desolate windswept landscape, though the hills on the far side of the valley were occasionally lit by snatches of sunlight. Blasts of wind still stopped me and sent me staggering sideways. Finding a campsite looked to be a real problem, as there was no shelter within sight, so I headed for a small area of forest the map showed a few miles to the northeast over a minor divide.

As I stumbled on through the tussocks and moss-filled watery holes, blown every which way by the wind, I realized the walk was almost over. I wouldn't go back up into the mountains. As soon as these thoughts occurred, I thought of life beyond the walk. My feelings were contradictory. I wanted both to finish as quickly as possible and to prolong the walk. But in my heart it was over, a feeling that I knew would not change. Completing the walk would be both a success and a challenge, an ending and a beginning.

On reaching a slight ridge I saw no sign of trees, just mile after mile of open, flat, mossy terrain. A closer examination of the country revealed the dark slash of a gravel bank alongside pools that looked as though it might offer a smidgen of shelter. I headed the half mile east to it. Before I got there rain began, light at first, then torrential.

The shallow stream course below the bank, barely worthy of the name valley, offered little protection from the wind. I tried to pitch the tarp against a gravel mound, but the wind quickly tore out the stakes and threatened to tear the flapping nylon from my grasp or rip it to shreds, so I abandoned the attempt. A long scout revealed no better spot to camp, so I pitched the tent on a flat patch of soft, shifting gravel, placing rocks on every stake. Nonetheless, gusts of wind pulled out stakes several times during the evening, making me dash outside to replace them and reinforce them with larger rocks.

By the time the tent was up, my hands and feet were numb and I was beginning to shiver. For the first time on the walk, I cooked in the tent vestibule and stored my food inside. There was no way I could cook and eat outside in this storm. My pack stayed outside under its cover, weighed down with rocks. The small vestibule was crowded with wet boots and clothing, and I had to cook very carefully. Every so often a gust of wind shook the tent and had me ready to hurl the stove outside. The temperature inside was forty-one degrees, and once I'd donned dry socks and long underwear, slid into the sleeping bag, and had a hot meal, I began to feel comfortably warm again.

Consulting the maps, I realized this might be the last wilderness camp of the walk. It was, as I wrote that night in my journal, "almost certainly the last in the Yukon, which I entered so long ago on the shores of Lake Bennett. Tomorrow I will enter the Northwest Territories, and my journey through the Yukon will be over. Today was a savage finale to the walk indeed." It wasn't over yet though, and the worst was still to come.

The night was wild, the heavy rain and strong winds continuing, and I did no more than doze, keeping my clothes on in case I had to abandon camp in the dark. The possibility of the tent's collapsing worried me, though not as much as it would have if this hadn't already happened a couple of times in the past. While knowing what to do if the worst happened was good for my peace of mind, knowing what a desperate chore it was did nothing for my cheerfulness. Toward morning the wind eased and I fell gratefully asleep, to wake at 8:30 to calm and an unusual pale light. The tent was sagging badly. I reached out a hand and pushed the walls. There was a brief slithering and suddenly it was much lighter. I knew the reason immediately. Several inches of wet snow covered the tent, pushing the fly sheet against the inner, and about a foot was piled up around the edge. Outside it was still snowing, and my pack was completely buried.

An urgent need to defecate forced me outside. I was reading William Golding's *Close Quarters* the night before and had noted what his protagonist had written in his journal: "'Moreover the calls of nature pay no attention to such trifles as a cracked head!'" Nor to snowfalls!

I dug out the pack and reset the tent, brushing the snow off the fly sheet. Then came the delicate task of reentering the tent without bringing in lots of snow. Moving the pans and stove into the inner tent, I placed the two food bags outside by the door. Then I hurriedly removed my wet rain jacket, backed into the tent, and sat on my Therm-a-Rest, quickly zipping the fly-sheet door to keep out the snow. Boots off, I removed my wet socks and long pants before slipping back into the still-warm sleeping bag. Inevitably, despite all my care, a little snow came in with me. I scooped up as much as I could and threw it out. My sleeping bag was already damp: the humidity was so high that keeping gear dry was just about impossible. Cooking inside didn't help, though it was essential. The tent filled with clouds of steam that then condensed on the walls. I had walked through the seasons. This was a winter camp.

With wet snow falling steadily and minimal visibility, there seemed no point in moving on. Walking would be very difficult, as would finding another campsite. This storm had been raging for sixty hours—first with rain, then strong winds that sprang up some twenty-five hours later; and now with their dissipation had come at least seven hours of snow. Overall I preferred the snow. It built up quickly on the tent, blocking both light and sound. The silence kept making me think the snow had stopped, but once I banged the walls I could hear clearly the gentle patter on the fly sheet, soft but insistent.

By early afternoon I was beginning to worry that the depth of snow would make walking difficult. I was also bored and frustrated, so I decided to try to reach the highway, which I estimated to be no more than eight to twelve miles away. Outside it was virtually a whiteout, and I walked north on a compass bearing. Despite the poor visibility the light was very bright, and I wore for the first time the dark glasses I had carried all the way from Dyea. There was now about a foot of soft wet snow on the ground, enough to completely hide the terrain and make walking extremely strenuous. The biggest problem was my feet. I had to cross a number of half-hidden willow-lined creeks, and I stepped repeatedly into unseen water-filled holes and dips. My feet were soon soaked and painfully cold.

After three and a half hours and, I guessed, very little mileage, I stopped on the bank of a creek I had just crossed, kicked out a flatish spot, and pitched the tent. It took an hour. My legs were tired and my feet were screaming with pain. I wanted to get camp set up before the temperature dropped. Despite the arduous slog through the wet snow, my clothes were dry under my waterproofs, testifying to the efficiency of Sympatex and Craghoppers's clever design. Only the wrists of my sweater were damp.

During the evening the sky began to clear and the snow stopped. A golden eagle flew low over the tent, a fine and cheering sight. I didn't know exactly where or when I had left the Yukon, but I was now definitely in the Northwest Territories, the border between the two running west to east here, and at most seven or eight miles south of the road. This, I was sure, really would be my last wilderness camp. I had achieved my aim and walked across the Yukon from south to north. I felt no sense of triumph, though. My concerns were to escape the snow and reach the highway. Feelings of achievement would come later.

The lull in the storm, for that's all it was, was soon over and more snow began to fall. Instead of the hard frost I had hoped for, the thermometer fell only to thirty-two, about the worst temperature for camping as everything becomes damp. It is much easier to keep warm at fifteen degrees. The wet, not the cold, was the problem. I slept in my thermal underwear and my only pair of dry socks. My sleeping bag was damp and the fill had packed into hard balls, losing its insulating power. The inner surface of the groundsheet was wet too, so I lay curled up, trying to stay on the Therm-a-Rest. I lit a candle to try to dry out the air a little, and after I had finished cooking I left the stove on for a few minutes to clear the steam. I really needed the door open to let out the moisture-laden air, but every time I undid the zipper snow poured in.

The eventual effects of the continuing storm on my state of mind were interesting. The immediate present became all important; I felt totally isolated from the world outside the little snow-swept piece of wilderness I was in. Thoughts of the walk, of home, of Fort McPherson became unreal.

A desperate five-and-a-half-hour slog through ankle- to thigh-deep snow, during which I slipped and slid over the slick, snow-covered tussocks and fell constantly into drifts, pools, and creeks, led next morning to the Dempster Highway. The weather grew steadily worse, with a cold wind and driving snow and hail. My feet were bitterly cold, and I lost all feeling in them whenever I stopped. For the last two hours I could see the highway winding down from Richardson Mountain Pass through rolling clouds. As I stumbled toward the road I felt strangely elated. I had walked the Yukon. My adventure was over.

There's a land—oh, it beckons and
beckons,
And I want to go back—and I will.
—Robert Service, "The
Spell of the Yukon"

10

Journey
Home

As I staggered the last few hundred yards of snow-covered tussocks to the highway, a pickup truck slowed and stopped, waiting for me. I had no doubts. I would take the lift. I was no longer in the Yukon, and walking the highway to Fort McPherson now seemed pointless. To turn down such an opportunity would have been madness—I could have waited hours for a vehicle to pass, yet one was stopping before I had even reached the road. All of a sudden the walk was over and the transition back to a world of motor transport and speed abruptly begun.

The heat inside the pickup was overwhelming. My clothes began to steam gently and warmth to trickle back into my toes. A burly figure sat behind the wheel. He didn't seem surprised to see me. He had stopped because, as he said, anyone out in this weather just had to want a ride. Originally from Nova Scotia, Ron (I never learned his last name) had been up here nine years and gave the impression he had seen so much that was unusual that nothing would surprise him now, certainly not an Englishman stumbling about in the snow. He was heading for Eagle Plains, looking en route for the first signs of the annual fall barren-ground-caribou migration, when the huge, 165,000-strong Porcupine herd crosses the highway on the way to its winter feeding grounds in the Richardson and Ogilvie mountains. He had found tracks that were a day or so old but hadn't seen any animals yet.

As we started the climb to Richardson Mountain Pass, the truck began to slip on the icy road, and Ron decided it would be wiser to return to Inuvik, where he lived. I didn't mind, as long as we ended up somewhere warm and dry.

The scenery flashed past. We soon left the mountains behind. Ferries took us across the wide Peel and Mackenzie rivers. Wooden drying racks stacked with salmon lined the banks, an age-old Indian way of preserving food for the winter. I took in little of it. Everything went by too fast. I was still trying to assimilate the abrupt ending of my summer in the wilderness. Ron told me many tales of traveling and hunting in the area as we sped on through flat country forested with black spruce. He had come up for a temporary job but was so taken with the North that he had stayed. The harshness of the wilderness appealed to him, though he said he was always well prepared, carrying in the truck firewood, a canvas tent, arctic boots, a thick padded shirt, overalls, rifles, food, and other camping and survival items. In winter, seven months long up here, he traveled the wilderness by snowmobile, towing his gear on a toboggan, hunting and fishing. "I believe in living off the land," he said. He was scornful of civilization and hated crowded places, telling me he had visited Europe when he was in the Canadian Air Force and would never go back. For him this was a last frontier, a last place where he could be free.

We passed through the small scattering of houses on the Peel River that is Fort McPherson, originally set up in 1840 as a Hudson's Bay Company trading post. Ron said there was no accommodation available, so I stayed with him to the end of the Dempster in Inuvik—"Place of Man" in the Inuit language—a modern town of three thousand people built in the late 1950s. I checked into the

Mackenzie Hotel for two nights. I needed to spend a day alone coming to terms with the sudden change in my existence before starting the long trek home. It was Saturday, so I couldn't collect the mail I was expecting at Fort McPherson until the following Monday. The hotel reception staff said they would try to arrange a lift south for me, standard practice it seemed.

After a day spent dawdling in Inuvik, which was like any other small modern town and had little of interest to offer visitors, I was ready to go home. Suddenly I wanted to see friends again, to talk and laugh with companions over coffee and beer, to sleep in my own bed, to be in a place I knew well. For now I no longer needed new wilderness vistas. For now.

I thought Inuvik out of place, an inappropriate scar in this vast timeless Arctic wilderness. There was no sense of its being in any way connected to its environment, no sense of its having grown out of its surrounding. Instead it appeared to have been dumped there, almost by accident. I felt that the mentality that planned Inuvik was the same unthinking one that trashed the Yukon with derelict mining camps and garbage-strewn hunting camps, a mentality that saw the wilderness as an enemy to be overcome rather than as a place of exquisite beauty and wonder. The physical consequences of this attitude had dogged my walk. Inuvik seemed to sum it up.

To be fair to Inuvik, I was not in a receptive frame of mind. I felt numb and drained, stunned at the walk's being over. This sense of anticlimax would pass, I knew, but I was glad I didn't know anyone there and could adjust to the new reality alone. It was quicker that way.

"There's a guy heading south tomorrow. You pay for the gas and he'll give you a ride." I accepted. A young, fair-haired man turned up in the lobby. "Hi, I'm Joe," he said. We shook hands. He was from Alabama but had recently started working in a hospital in Alaska. He was eager to get to Dawson in one push, so we left straightaway in his Toyota pickup, heading south in convoy with another truck, driven by a Los Angeles policeman named Paul. The storm had passed, and the snow-clad mountains sparkled in the sun. We stopped at Richardson Mountain Pass. The sign welcoming travelers to the Yukon showed the gold-rush stampeders climbing the Chilkoot Pass, now an image from my past too. Another sign bore some wise words:

> You are welcome here, traveller. Enjoy this land with the understanding that it has been left briefly in your trust for the benefit of future generations.

As good tourists, we also paused at the Arctic Circle. It was only ten days since I had drunk coffee here with the Japanese round-the-world-traveler, but it seemed another lifetime. Eagle Plains seemed familiar yet strange. Places change when you arrive in a different way. I collected my goods and we sped on, past the fall colors of the Eagle Plains hills, past the place where I had seen the wolves, past the Ogilvie River and the Ogilvie Mountains, Engineer Creek, Mount Distincta, past my life in the northern Yukon. I stared through the window and said farewell in my heart. I felt very sad. Suddenly every second of the walk, every yellow fall leaf, every shining stone on a creek bed, every distant mountain peak, every campsite, every drop of rain, every blackfly, every squelchy muskeg pool was infinitely precious to me, and I wanted to hold on to every one intensely and never let it go. To do so, I felt, would break my heart.

My reverie was shattered abruptly at North Fork Pass when, at the very point where I had joined the Dempster a month before, the truck spun off the road, somersaulted two times and came to rest upside down in the muskeg. Or so I am told. I remember none of this, presumably because I received a knock on the head at some point, though Joe told me my eyes stayed open. I came to in a speeding, rocking ambulance with an oxygen mask over my face. The paramedics were asking me my address, and the effort of having to spell the Scottish words for them seemed to bring me around.

Until then, apparently, I had not been able to remember anything at all about who or where I was, though I had helped Joe unload the truck, insisting that I take my cameras and film with me. Joe was relieved when I started to respond. I felt sorry for him. At least I hadn't had to worry about anyone. It wasn't his fault anyway. At the time he didn't know why he had gone off the road, but later he wrote to tell me the cause had been a burst tire.

I returned to Dawson strapped to a stretcher, though I felt much better than when I had walked in the first time with a stinking head cold. A doctor, hauled out of his bed, for it was now late at night, muttered "concussion" but said I could go. Totally confused, I found myself out in the streets of Dawson in the rain. I had my fleece jacket on, but my other clothing and all my belongings were in my pack, and I didn't know where that was. I had been told that Joe was in the Triple J Hotel, so I headed there and checked in. Paul appeared and said he felt like having a beer, "and you look like you need one." So, well after midnight, we wandered around Dawson having last drinks in Diamond Tooth Gertie's and a few other places. I felt completely detached from reality.

The next day it was as if the accident had never happened. The end of the previous day was a weird blur. I accepted Joe's account of what had happened, but I had only vague memories of it. Filling in an accident form at the police station and recovering my gear convinced me something had happened, though I wasn't sure what. I stayed in Dawson the rest of the day, reflecting on the irony of surviving all the supposed perils of the wilderness, the bears and creek fords and steep cliffs and swamps that I had been warned about, and then being wrecked on the highway. I would take the backcountry, grizzlies and all, anytime. It was civilization that was dangerous.

A bus ride to Whitehorse and I was back in the Regina Hotel where I had begun, again courtesy of Yukon Tourism. George and Ron welcomed me back, and George made a request. Would I give a short talk on my walk at a Yukon Rotary Club luncheon? Of course, I said. It was a strange occasion, at least to me. I outlined the highlights of the walk, then burbled about the beauties of the place to people who lived there. I also spoke to the *Yukon News* again and did a final interview for CBC. Then it was onto the plane, and the Yukon was a fading gray-green land far below—and soon, for me, a memory.

The hectic days immediately following the end of the walk had flashed past in a confusing melee. On the long flight home I finally had time to begin sorting out my thoughts and feelings. Although I hadn't reached the Arctic Ocean, a goal I always knew was probably out of reach, I had walked the Yukon from end to end. Much more important than tying the ends of the walk together neatly was the experience of a summer in the wilderness, making contact, however tentatively, with the world that sustains us and of which, however much our actions deny it, we are a part. The confusion and numbness passed, as did the desire to hang on to what had already gone. I felt relaxed and happy. I was going home content.

Appendixes

Chronology

25,000–10,000 B.C.   First humans enter the Yukon.

1789   Alexander Mackenzie mentions the Yukon River in his journals.

1826   Sir John Franklin becomes the first white man to enter the Yukon when he travels past the northern end of the Richardson Mountains on the second of his land-based expeditions in search of the Northwest Passage.

1835   Andrey Glazunov, a trader for the Russian American Company, becomes the first European to travel on the Yukon River.

1839   John Bell of the Hudson's Bay Company, in search of furs, explores the river in the northern Yukon later named after him.

1848   Robert Campbell of the Hudson's Bay Company establishes a trading post called Fort Selkirk at the confluence of the Yukon and Pelly rivers.

1852   Chilkat Indians from southeast Alaska burn Fort Selkirk.

1870   Canada purchases Rupert's Land, which included what was to become the Yukon Territory, from the Hudson's Bay Company.

1880   The first prospectors enter the Yukon via the Chilkoot Pass.

1883   Lieutenant Frederick Schwatka of the U.S. Army travels the

Yukon River from end to end, naming many of the places and landmarks along the way.

1887–88 George Dawson's Canadian Yukon Exploration Expedition.

1888 William Ogilvie, surveyor on Dawson's expedition, links the Yukon and Peel river drainages by an overland route.

1889 The trading post at Fort Selkirk (then called Campbell's Fort) is revived by Arthur Harper.

1891–95 Jack Dalton cuts a trail from the Lynn Canal to Fort Selkirk along the line of the Chilkat Indians' trade route.

1896 *August:* George Carmacks, Tagish Charlie, and Skookum Jim discover gold on Rabbit Creek (later renamed Bonanza Creek) in the Klondike.
Joseph Ladue stakes out the Dawson City town site.

1897 The Klondike gold rush begins when the *Excelsior* and the *Portland* arrive in San Francisco and Seattle, respectively, carrying gold.

1898 *February:* The North West Mounted Police open a customs post on the Chilkoot Pass.
April: More than sixty stampeders are killed in an avalanche.
May: Seven thousand boats set out down the Yukon River for the Klondike as the ice breaks up.
Dawson City becomes the capital of the Yukon Territory.

1899 *February:* White Pass and Yukon railroad opens.
July: Railroad reaches Whitehorse.

1906–09 Construction of the Twelve Mile Power Plant on the southern slopes of the Tombstone Range to provide power for the Klondike dredges.

1911 Four Mounties, the Lost Patrol, disappear while on winter patrol between Fort McPherson and Dawson City.

1932 Albert Johnson shoots a policeman, and the hunt for the Mad Trapper of Rat River takes place in the Richardson Mountains.

1942 The Alaska Highway, first road through the Yukon, is built by the U.S. Army.

1953 Whitehorse replaces Dawson City as the Yukon's capital.

1979 Completion of the Dempster Highway, named for Inspector Jack Dempster of the Royal North West Mounted Police, who led the search for the Lost Patrol.

Facts and Figures

The route I actually walked turned out to be significantly different from the one I had planned, many decisions being made from day to day. I had a complete set of 1:50,000 topographic maps for the original route, but these maps do not cover a large area. In several places I wandered out of their range and had to use the 1:250,000 maps that I carried for an overview of the area. These instances occurred between Fort Selkirk and Dawson and between the Tombstone Recreation Park and the Eagle Plains Hotel. Although the maps were generally accurate, many were in black and white and outdated, not showing the Dempster Highway or even Fort McPherson. The landscape is on such a vast scale that while I often didn't know where in a valley I was, I always knew which valley I was in.

The route I walked went via Dyea–the Chilkoot Trail–Bennett Lake–Carcross–Caribou Mountain–Mount Lorne–Whitehorse–Takhini Hot Springs–Little River–Klusha Creek–Nordenskiöld River–Klondike Highway–Carmacks–Yukon Crossing–Yukon River–Fort Selkirk–(boat)–Pelly Farm–Black Creek–Walhalla Creek–Scroggie Creek–Stewart River–(boat)–McCrimmon Creek–Indian River–Eldorado

Creek–Dawson City–Midnight Dome–Lepine Creek–Ballarat Creek–
Little Twelve Mile River–Tombstone River–Talus Lake–Tombstone
Pass–Divide Lake–North Klondike River–Tombstone Recreation
Park–Lil Canyon–North Fork Pass–Dempster Highway–Mount Dis-
tincta–Windy Pass–Dempster Highway–Engineer Creek Recreational
Park–Ogilvie River–Transplant Mountain–headwaters of Whitestone
River–Dempster Highway–Eagle Plains Hotel–Arctic Circle–Mount
Hare–Cornwall River–Dempster Highway east of Richardson
Mountain Pass.

My extensive use of small-scale maps plus the many cross-country sections where I wandered widely make it impossible to work out
accurately the total distance walked. The sum of the distances given at
the head of each chapter is a conservative 850 miles. I estimate the real
distance at well over 1,000 miles.

The whole adventure lasted 83 days, though I walked on only 68
of these—an average, taking 850 miles as the total, of 12½ miles a day.
In practice this amount varied widely: I usually did 20 or more miles a
day when on roads, often less than 10 when traveling cross-country. I
walked approximately 270 miles on paved or gravel roads, 50 miles on
good trails, and 530 miles cross-country or on hard-to-follow abandoned trails. Although I hiked a third of the distance on roads, the
faster pace the roads allowed meant that I spent only 17 days, a quarter
of my time, on roads. I spent 51 days in the wilderness.

I slept 67 nights in the tent and 16 in cabins, motels, or other
buildings. Fifty-six camps were in the wilderness, the rest on campgrounds.

Food

Food is of paramount importance on a wilderness walk. I knew from previous treks that food needs to be palatable as well as nutritious. When you're living on freeze-dried and dehydrated rations for weeks on end, it's easy to tire of them. AlpineAire meals are my favorite specialty backpacking food, so the company sent supplies from California to Whitehorse for me.

AlpineAire meals are additive-free and based on whole foods. As I don't usually eat meat, I chose vegetarian soups and entrees. All the meals were simple to prepare, requiring just the addition of boiling water and then a seven-to-ten-minute wait, a boon in bad weather or when I was tired and hungry. The "no cook" meals helped save on stove fuel. The meals are lightweight, around 7 ounces a packet, provide plenty of calories (about 625 per entree), come in crushproof sealed foil packets, and—most important of all—are very tasty. I never tired of them, though by the end of the trip I did have favorites, in particular Alpine Minestrone soup and Pasta Roma.

Breakfasts were simple, usually just granola, or when I ran out, stewed dried fruit, with coffee and fruit juice. Each day I ate lunch as a series of snacks consisting of a variety of granola-and-dried-fruit bars, trail mix, and a couple of Bear Valley MealPack bars, which are made from grains, dried fruit, nuts, honey, fruit juice, nonfat milk, and other natural ingredients. I found the bars delicious. When I ran low on bars I had soup for lunch.

Overall the food was sufficient, though after the first few weeks my appetite soared and I had to appease it with extra items such as cheese and chocolate. Whenever there was a café or store, I filled up with fresh food; many people I met en route gave me fresh food as well.

I've never decided whether multivitamins are needed on a long walk or not. I had taken them on previous summerlong treks, but this time I didn't bother. The powdered fruit drinks I carried (Energen C) were high in Vitamin C, but they didn't prevent the only illness I suffered, a severe cold between Fort Selkirk and Dawson.

Equipment

Equipment for a venture into remote wilderness must be reliable, especially when the trek is summerlong, so I took great care with my selection. Some of the gear was new, some well used. All of it was top quality, carefully balanced between durability and weight.

Shelter

My tent was a Phoenix Phreeranger, a roomy single-hoop model whose weight of just 4 pounds makes it ideal for the solo backpacker. I had used this tent on previous long walks, so I knew it was easy to pitch and would cope well with winds, heavy rain, and snow. In addition to a vestibule, the tent has an insect-netting inner door. This proved vital for keeping out mosquitoes and blackflies.

Because of the presence of both black and grizzly bears in the Yukon wilderness, I cooked and ate well away from my sleeping site in case the smell of my food attracted them. As so few people travel the Yukon wilderness, there isn't the bear problem common to such popular places as Yosemite National Park. Even so, it wasn't worth taking risks. In good weather, eating away from my tent was no problem, but during storms eating outside is no fun, so I carried a nylon tarp, along with a few guylines and stakes, to fashion a cooking shelter. I needed it so often that it was well worth its 1-pound weight. At times I used both my staff and camera tripod as makeshift poles to support the tarp.

For nighttime warmth I took a Mountain Equipment Lightline down-filled sleeping bag, which packs very small and weighs just 2 pounds 2½ ounces. Overnight lows in the tent ran from 60 to 21 degrees Fahrenheit, a range the Lightline coped with well, being cool enough when unzipped on hot nights and warm enough with the hood pulled up tight on cold ones. I always use a down bag on long walks because of the low weight and bulk, but down must be dry to be effective, so I packed the Lightline in a stuff sack and then in a waterproof nylon pack liner.

Because of the permafrost, a good insulating mat was essential. Comfort is important too. As on other walks, I carried a 17-ounce Therm-a-Rest Backpacker Ultra-Lite self-inflating mat. This kept me warm and helped iron out the bumps and stones on which I frequently had to sleep.

Cooking

When I learned it was possible to light a fire at most of my campsites, I bought a Coghlan's Camp Grill in Whitehorse. I used it enough for it to be worth its 10½ ounces.

Most of the time I used the same 12-ounce MSR WhisperLite Internationale stove that I had used for four and a half months in the Canadian Rockies in 1988. Again it performed well. Although it will run on kerosene, I used Coleman Fuel or similar in it, as this gas is cleaner and easier to use. A pint-capacity MSR fuel bottle doubled as the fuel tank, with extra fuel carried in a quart Sigg bottle. I found, as on other trips, that a quart of fuel lasted ten days.

I'm a recent convert to stainless steel rather than aluminum for pans (steel is easier to clean, more durable, and doesn't taint food). My cook set consisted of a 1-quart stainless steel Olicamp pot and a pint-size stainless steel Cascade Cup. I used the cup as both a second pan and a mug. The two together weighed 12 ounces. The rest of my kitchen consisted of a soup spoon, a teaspoon, a Nalgene 1-quart water bottle, a small Opinel folding knife, and a 2-gallon collapsible nylon water bag, total weight again 12 ounces. North of Dawson I carried a second quart bottle so I could easily carry water to dry camps.

Footwear

Having very broad feet (caused by carrying heavy loads, according to some!) I chose Vasque Summit boots for the trip, which are available in a wide fit. A medium-weight (3½ pounds for my size 9½'s) one-piece leather boot, the Summits were very comfortable and supportive and still in surprisingly good condition at the end of the walk. They weren't even in need of resoling.

I find a change of footwear essential on a long walk despite the extra weight, and I carried a pair of New Balance Trailbuster running shoes for campwear, stream fords, and road walking (weight 1 pound 9 ounces).

I had three changes of socks, two pairs being traditional Ragg wool (Ryla and Janus brands), the other Thor-Lo-Padd trekking socks. All three pairs survived the walk, but overall I found the Thor-Lo-Padd socks the most comfortable.

Clothing

My clothing had to cope with conditions ranging from hot sunshine to blizzards and be tough enough to stand up to weeks of bushwhacking. To deal with this variety of conditions I used, as always, the layer system. A pair of Patagonia Baggies shorts was my basic garment, worn whenever the weather was kind enough and the bushwhacking wasn't too severe.

Most of my clothing was made by the British outdoor-clothing company Craghoppers. My T-shirt, which I wore every day, was made from Diolen Sportant Fresh polyester. It wicked moisture very quickly, was cool in the heat—and barely smelled at all, even when worn continuously for three weeks without being washed. I also had long johns in the same thin stretchy material and a sweater made of a thicker version, both of which I wore frequently during the colder weather of the last few weeks.

For warm wear I had a Craghoppers Tarn jacket, made from Akzo's Diolen polyester Sportant Fleece. This lightweight (18 ounces) garment proved very warm when worn under a shell jacket (like most fleece, it's not windproof) and was all I needed for most of the walk. I also used it as a pillow every night and frequently as a towel. Despite this (mis)use, it finished the trip in good condition.

When it was too cool for shorts or when I didn't want my legs shredded by prickly vegetation, I wore 50/50 polycotton Craghoppers Trail Pants. They were light, windproof, quick drying, and comfortable, but they eventually became torn due to the constant bushwhacking, and some of the seams split (one of which I crudely stitched up for decency's sake before I reached Dawson!). In fairness, I doubt any other lightweight cotton-mix pants would have lasted longer.

Instead of a shirt I took a windproof jacket made up for me by Craghoppers in a lightweight polyester microfiber fabric. Along with the T-shirt, I wore this upper garment most, using it as an outer shell in cold, windy, dry weather, to protect my arms when bushwhacking, when biting insects were a problem, and also as a shirt in camp when the fleece top was too warm.

My rain jacket was a Craghoppers Cloudbreaker jacket, which has a polycotton outer shell and a Sympatex lining. Because of the polycotton, the Cloudbreaker is comfortable and quiet, and the Sympatex kept out rain and snow while allowing moisture vapor to pass through. The jacket performed excellently and finished the walk as waterproof and breathable as it began.

Less often worn were my Craghoppers Sympatex/Tactel rain pants with full-length zippers, though at times they were essential. I found they worked best when worn over the long johns rather than the trail pants.

On the second half of the walk I backed up my fleece- and thermalwear with an ultralight RAB Kinder down-filled sweater. I needed it only a few times, but it was well worth its 18 ounces and minimum bulk on those occasions.

I also carried polypro thermal gloves, pile mitts, and a knitted acrylic hat for cool weather, plus a Tilley hat for the sun. I ended up using the hat far more than I expected, as it is so comfortable, unlike most hats. Made of white canvas, it shed rain, kept off the sun, and when sprayed with repellent helped keep bugs away from my face.

Accessories

The accessories list seems to go on and on! However, nothing I carried was superfluous. Perhaps the most unusual item was a walking staff, but I find one essential when carrying a heavy load over rough terrain, as I was most of the time. Mine is an aluminum model, Cascade Designs's Tracks Chief of Staffs. Being collapsible, it fits inside my pack for air transport.

Other accessories consisted of a Gregson first-aid kit, a Silva Type 3 compass, a Petzl Zoom headlamp, 30 yards of nylon parachute cord, sunglasses, a small repair kit, a Baggins nylon zip-around Pocket Office holding documents and writing materials, a max/min thermometer, Sirius 8 x 21 minibinoculars, a mosquito head net, Bug Off insect repellent, a toilet trowel, a bandanna, a wash kit, sunscreen, and toilet paper.

Pack

The total weight of all this equipment came to 45 pounds, of which about 5 pounds was worn on most days, leaving 40 pounds to be carried. Together with 10 pounds of camera gear plus 2 pounds of food a day, that made for a load of 70 pounds at the start of a ten-day section, a horrendous weight that meant I needed the best pack I could find. Despite trying out new designs, I ended up taking my five-year-old, 7,630-cubic-inch, internal-frame Gregory Cassin, the most comfortable heavy-load backpack I know. It performed superbly throughout the walk.

I also wore a small fanny pack, the Pod Hipsac, so that I had easy access to frequently needed items like maps, compass, camera, film, lens filters, binoculars, notebook, and more.

Photography

Photographically the walk presented a challenge because of the prohibitive weight of a fully equipped gadget bag. Careful consideration produced a selection of gear that will seem minimal to most photographers but proved to be just adequate.

On a long trek in remote country it is too great a risk to take only one camera body. Twice in the past, problems have developed that could have cost thousands of photographs if I hadn't had a spare body, so I always carry two SLR bodies, each loaded with a different film. Having tried other brands, I now use Nikons for their durability and because you can use all the lenses with all the bodies, auto-focus or not.

While the professional Nikon F4 is undoubtedly a fine camera, it's far too heavy to lug around the wilderness. Instead I took the much lighter N8008, which, apart from the weight, has one feature the F4 lacks that is essential for the solo walker. This is the 30-second self-timer. When there's no other human being within miles and you need a person in a picture for purposes of scale or to break up a monotonous foreground, then you have to use yourself. Too many pictures of a blurred body caught in the act of dashing into the scene or, if in place, looking breathless and uncomfortable have taught me the limitations of a 10-second timer. The N8008's timer was a joy to use. I even managed to photograph myself lying in the tent fully zipped into my sleeping bag!

Although the N8008 can set the exposure automatically I usually used manual settings for greater control. I seldom used the auto-focus function, it being useless for landscape photography where depth of field is of major importance.

My second camera was a manual FM2, taken because it isn't dependent on batteries or complex electronics. It is also lightweight and durable. The two cameras are completely different, but I used both most days and switched easily from one to the other.

Deciding to take two camera bodies was easy; deciding on the lenses to accompany them was much harder. After much thought I settled for a Nikkor 35–70 F3.3–5.6 AF zoom as my general-purpose lens and a Sigma UC 70–210 F4.5–5.6 AF zoom as my telephoto, the latter chosen because it is far lighter than the Nikon equivalent. I also wanted both fast and wide-angle lenses, needs I combined by taking a Nikkor 24mm F2.8 AF lens. Finally, for photographing wildlife I took a Tamron 2x converter, bought at the last minute and not tried out before the walk.

Photographs of nature should look natural. Filters, therefore, did not take up much room in my pack. The only one I use much is a polarizer, but it is so important that I carried two. I also carried a graduated gray filter for reducing the contrast between bright skies and dark land, but I rarely used it. The only others were the skylight filters I keep on my lenses at all times except when using a polarizer.

Whenever possible I use a tripod, both to obtain sharp pictures and as a composition aid. It was also essential for self-portraits and low-light pictures. Finding a tripod that combined at least a degree of stability with light weight was very difficult, but I finally decided on a Cullman 2101 model at 1 pound 6 ounces. It proved both functional and tough. Despite being strapped to the outside of the pack when not in use, it survived the walk intact. It did need weighing down in strong winds, and I wouldn't like to use it with a heavy telephoto lens, but it was a good compromise.

I used Fujichrome film, both ISO 100 and 50. I took the "amateur" version because I couldn't guarantee cold storage—the film went ahead in my supply boxes, which could have been stored in sunshine or next to a heater for weeks. Also, as the processing is prepaid, I could mail batches of film back to a lab in Britain, which then sent it home to be viewed and checked. Every so often I could then learn how the pictures were turning out. I hoped thereby to avoid losing too many pictures if a camera or lens was malfunctioning. I used the medium-speed film for hand-held shots and the finer-grained slow film for tripod photographs. I kept the N8008 loaded with ISO 100 film and the FM2 with ISO 50. I also carried a few rolls of Fujichrome 400, which I used for photographing the northern lights.

Despite having two camera bodies, I still took great care of them and always kept them in well-padded and incredibly tough Camera Care Systems bags. I slung the N8008 across my body in a CCS AF Tusker bag that protected it from rain, snow, dust, and regular thrashings by dense bushes and small trees. To make the carry as comfortable as possible, I attached a wide, stretchy Op-Tech strap to the Tusker. An ordinary CCS SLR case carried the FM2, which resided in the top pocket of my pack, while the lenses stayed in CCS lens cases carried in the fanny pack. I kept filters, film, cable release, and cleaning materials there too, and a small but essential notebook for recording details of the pictures I took. Too often in the past I've sat for hours staring at a photograph trying to work out exactly where it was taken.

The total weight of my equipment, excluding film, was 9 pounds —very light for an SLR system.

I returned home to find 66 boxes of transparencies waiting to be viewed and filed. Going through them showed me what had worked and what hadn't. As always most of the failures (and there are always failures; I wouldn't believe any photographer who didn't admit to them) were mine rather than the equipment's. My minimal kit did let me down on telephoto shots using the converter. Their quality simply isn't good enough for anything other than personal viewing for memory's sake. The combination of the F5.6 210-end of the zoom lens with a converter didn't work. Even without the converter I had found the dark viewfinder image and the necessarily slow shutter speeds a problem at times. But a faster or a longer lens would have meant more weight. The lenses themselves all produced fine results.

Glenview Public Library
1930 Glenview Road
Glenview, ILL

Further Reading

I read or referred to the following books before, during, and after the walk. Each is about the North in some way, though some of them may seem only obliquely related to walking in the Yukon. Suffice it to say that I found them all worth reading and would recommend them to anyone seeking to learn more about the wilderness of the far north.

Amundsen, Roald. *The North West Passage*. London: Constable & Co., 1908.

Anderson, F. W. *The Death of Albert Johnson, Mad Trapper of Rat River*. Surrey, B.C.: Heritage House Publishing Company Ltd., 1986. The story of the Mad Trapper of Rat River.

Berton, Pierre. *Klondike: The Last Great Gold Rush*. Toronto: McClelland & Stewart, 1987. A superb, detailed account.

Calef, George. *Journey the Dempster Highway: A Traveller's Guide to the Land and Its People*. Whitehorse, Yukon: Yukon Conservation Society, 1984. Well-illustrated guide with an emphasis on natural history.

Coates, Ken S. and William R. Morrison. *Land of the Midnight Sun: A*

History of the Yukon. Edmonton, Alberta: Hurtig Publishers Ltd., 1988. Comprehensive.

Coutts, R. C. *Yukon: Places and Names*. Sydney, B.C.: Gray's Publishing Ltd., 1980. A fascinating reference book.

Dawson Indian Band. *Han Indians: People of the River.* Whitehorse, Yukon: Dawson Indian Band, 1988. Interesting booklet about the history and culture of the Han Indians. Available from Macs on Main or Fireweed in Whitehorse.

Frisch, Robert. *Birds by the Dempster Highway.* Whitehorse, Yukon: Yukon Conservation Society, 1987. A list of what you might see.

Herrero, Stephen. *Bear Attacks: Their Causes and Avoidance.* Piscataway, N.J.: Nick Lyons Books/Winchester Press, 1985. As much as you could possibly want to know.

Holloway, Samuel D. *Yukon Gold: A Guide for the Modern Goldseeker.* Whitehorse, Yukon: Outcrop (Yukon) Ltd., 1985. Enthusiastic account of current prospecting practices; useful information, if rather disturbing for the wilderness lover.

Jones, Tim. *The Last Great Race: The Iditarod.* Harrisburg, Pa.: Stackpole Books, 1988. An exciting insight into long-distance dogsled racing.

Karpes, A. C.(Gus). *The Upper Yukon River*, 2 vols. Whitehorse, Yukon: Kugh Enterprises, 1986. Intended for the canoeist, but contains many interesting anecdotes and snippets of local history.

Lanz, Walter. *Along the Dempster: An Outdoor Guide to Canada's Northernmost Highway.* Vancouver, B.C.: Oak House Publishing, 1990. Lavishly illustrated guide to walks and canoe trips accessible from the Dempster.

London, Jack. *The Call of the Wild* and *White Fang.* Classic tales, if rather unfair to wolves!

Lopez, Barry. *Arctic Dreams.* New York: Charles Scribner's Sons, 1986. In praise of the North. A wonderful book.

McCready, Marina. *Gateway to Gold: Skagway, the White Pass, and the Chilkoot Trail.* Whitehorse, Yukon: Studio North Ltd., 1990. Photographic study.

Muir, John. *The Eight Wilderness-Discovery Books.* Seattle: The Mountaineers, 1992. Includes *Travels in Alaska.*

Newman, Peter C. *Caesars of the Wilderness.* Toronto: Penguin Books,

1987. The fascinating story of the Hudson's Bay Company.

North, Dick. *The Mad Trapper of Rat River.* Toronto: Macmillan Paperbacks, 1987. An enthralling account.

—. *The Lost Patrol.* Anchorage: Alaska Northwest, 1978. Chilling.

—. *Jack London's Cabin.* Yukon: Jack London Series, 1986. Booklet on the search for the remains of the cabin London lived in during the gold rush.

Patterson, R. M. *Dangerous River.* Chelsea, Vt.: Chelsea Green, 1992. Exciting adventures on the Nahanni River in the 1920s.

Satterfield, Archie. *Chilkoot Pass: The Most Famous Trail in the North.* Anchorage: Alaska Northwest Publishing Company, 1978. Covers both the gold rush and the modern trail.

Service, Robert. *The Best of Robert Service.* London: A & C Black, 1987.

Sheridan, Guy. *Tales of a Cross Country Skier.* Sparkford, England: Oxford Illustrated Press, 1987. Includes account of a long ski tour in the Yukon.

Stanley, David. *Alaska–Yukon Handbook.* Chico, Ca.: Moon Publications, 1984. Well-written tourist guide with much information on budget travel.

Townsend, Chris, *The Backpacker's Handbook.* Camden, Maine: Ragged Mountain Press, 1993. Covers equipment and techniques for wilderness walking.

—. *High Summer: Backpacking the Canadian Rockies.* Seattle: Cloudcap, 1989. Story of my end-to-end walk along this range.

Trelawny, John G. *Wildflowers of the Yukon, Alaska, and Northwestern Canada.* Victoria, B.C.: Sono Nis Press, 1988. Excellent field guide.

Yukon Fish and Wildlife Branch. *The Bear Facts.* Whitehorse, Yukon: Yukon Renewable Resources, 1987. A useful little booklet.

Most of the Yukon is protected only by its rapidly diminishing remoteness and inaccessibility. There are many threats to the continued integrity of this great wilderness. Those who are concerned may wish to contact:

Yukon Conservation Society
Box 4163, Whitehorse
Yukon, Canada, Y1A 3T3

3 1170 00362 6920